THE

ASTRAL CODEX

USING DREAMS & OUT-OF-BODY
EXPERIENCES ON A SPIRITUAL JOURNEY

BELSEBUUB

MYSTICAL LIFE
PUBLICATIONS

(handwritten margin notes):
energy line
- meditation, help
HP. or Guides
Evening
- concentration
+ visualization
+ Finish
w/
shield
- pray

The Astral Codex: Using Dreams and Out-of-Body
Experiences on a Spiritual Journey
By Belsebuub

Illustrations by Angela Pritchard

Published March 2016 by Mystical Life Publications Ltd
www.mysticallifepublications.org

ISBN: 978-0-9924113-2-9

First edition 2001, A Course in Astral Travel and Dreams. First published online in PDF format.

Second edition, A Course in Astral Travel and Dreams, 2004 hardcover ISBN 978-0-9740560-1-2, 2005 paperback ISBN 978-0-9740560-3-6, 2010 paperback ISBN 978-0-9789864-4-5.

Third edition 2006, When I Go to Sleep, paperback ISBN 978-0-9740560-8-1.

Fourth edition August 2013, The Astral Codex: Out-of-Body Experiences and Lucid Dreaming for Spiritual Knowledge, eBook (EPUB) ISBN 978-0-9873147-6-5, eBook (Kindle) ISBN 978-0-9873147-7-2.

Fifth edition March 2016, The Astral Codex: Using Dreams and Out-of-Body Experiences on a Spiritual Journey, paperback ISBN 978-0-9924113-2-9.

Belsebuub's official website: www.belsebuub.com

CONTENTS

CHAPTER ELEVEN

BAD DREAMS, NIGHTMARES, 127
AND SINISTER ENTITIES

CHAPTER TWELVE

SCIENTIFIC PROOF FOR 157
OUT-OF-BODY EXPERIENCES

CHAPTER ONE

AN INTRODUCTION

ASTRAL PROJECTION IS A NATURAL FUNCTION of the human body—every night we go into the astral plane unconsciously in dreams; astral projecting is simply going there consciously (which is going there knowing that you are leaving your physical body). It happens spontaneously to around 10 percent of the population, but it's possible to learn techniques to consciously be aware of the natural process of traveling out of the body into different dimensions, to learn to travel around the astral plane, and to seek out knowledge there on a regular basis.

The astral plane is the source of many of the premonitions, prophecies, visions, spiritual teachings, divine visitations, and symbolic artwork found in ancient spiritual texts and teachings.

Although not referred to in the terms we use today, out-of-body experiences have been written about throughout human history in terms specific to the time and culture, and are an innate part of human nature and experience.

Some in ancient texts were said to be "in the spirit" or "caught up," and dreams were a common source of spiritual guidance. Scenes similar to those depicted by ancient peoples throughout history can still be found when traveling out of the body in the astral plane and in near-death experiences today.

The symbolic content of ancient texts and the art of archaeological sites have often been misinterpreted as myths, legends, and the attempts of primitive peoples to understand their world, but many have their origin in the astral plane. The language of the astral plane is intuitive and symbolic, which is why many of the messages brought back by people who have astral travelled or dreamt are symbolic in their nature and have formed highly sophisticated symbolic artwork and texts such as those of ancient Egypt, India, and Latin America.

Since the astral plane is common to all of humankind, the symbols and writings of different unrelated cultures which existed at different times often have many similarities, share common symbols, and contain the same universal principles at their core. Life is multi-dimensional, and the astral plane is part of another dimension. This does not conflict with many religions, but actually explains much of their source and provides a background for their cosmologies.

From their texts and artwork it is clear that ancient peoples knew of the existence of the astral plane and used it, and they did so not for pleasure or entertainment, but as a means of acquiring spiritual knowledge, to assist them in the process of conscious awakening. I propose a return to that ancient way of learning for everyone interested in learning about truth in life.

The astral plane is humanity's connection to spiritual realms and guidance; we all go there at death as our stay here is just temporary, but we also go there every night with dreams. Spiritual seekers throughout time have understood this connection and used it to get spiritual guidance to help them in their own spiritual journey and bring back knowledge to help people here.

The astral plane is a real dimension beyond time and the body, where other beings and forces of light and darkness exist, which all have their influence upon the world here completely unbeknownst to most. By using the astral plane for spiritual knowledge we can find out what is really behind what is going on in the world today and get answers to some of the most profound questions of life, such as why we are here, where do we come from, and what happens after death—from our own direct spiritual experience. Many of these experiences in the astral plane and higher realms formed the basis of religious teachings that became the beliefs of many. Yet anyone today can leave their body and get their own experience of higher realities.

To have out-of-body experiences (OBEs) when you want to requires learning the right kinds of techniques; most of the effective ones have been used by people around the world since antiquity. The techniques are actually able to go far deeper into the experience of travel out of the body than the methods of conventional science, since science is limited by its methods in an area of study that by its nature is nonphysical and based on inner personal experience.

I and many others who have practiced the information in this book have even been able to meet other people in the astral plane who were also traveling there and to verify the meeting with them when awake again in the physical world. We've also been able to verify the existence of many of the things written about in sacred texts and even meet some of the beings they refer to. It's possible to take part in real events that occur in the astral plane, some of which are to do with a person's own spiritual development, learning, and progress, and are extremely valuable for someone who is interested in spiritual awakening.

The mysteries of life and death are revealed in stages according to a person's capacity to understand them and according to a person's inner spiritual level. This is why many can learn to travel in the astral plane, some on a fairly regular basis, but few ever penetrate its mysteries. To do that requires much more than learning how to astral travel, and in this book, I give an explanation of the broader context of astral travel for those who wish to use it for a higher purpose.

THE WIDER CONTEXT OF ASTRAL TRAVEL

Astral projection is a way to understand some of the nature of consciousness and its experience of the multi-dimensional universe. Astral experiences can help you to explore not only other dimensions, but also your inner self too. You can discover hidden layers of yourself you never knew existed, and with that understanding you can change. You can also be taught about yourself, what you need to change, steps you can take in your life, and learn about mistakes you're making, about future events affecting your life, and your dreams can become a great source of learning too.

To be outside the body can be a profound experience, even life-changing. Many people after having an out-of-body experience for the first time relate how they were changed in their perception of who they are and what life was, after feeling what it was to look back at their body and realize that they were more than their body and life was more than just the material world. This kind of experience can open someone up to the realms of higher consciousness and the incredible potential that awaits us. In this book I not only explain about the astral world, but also show that it's possible to get there, to travel and open the doors to that incredible but latent potential, which every human being has the ability to realize.

Astral travel helps us to understand our context in life as human beings living on earth, and allows us to see that we exist in a multi-dimensional universe. Each of us at our root is consciousness, and in the highest of the spiritual realms life and form become light. I experienced this in an OBE in which I went to the outer ring of the source of creation. In the experience, instead of feeling like I was coming out of my body I seemed to collapse in upon myself, as though being swallowed by a black hole that was not black, but a pure and total light. I erupted into an existence where there is only light which has no shadows, and I as a thinking and feeling person was reduced to consciousness, or rather expanded into it—and in the light, which was life as consciousness, everything existed.

This was a very temporary experience which occurred in a higher realm than the astral plane. It happened not in astral projection but through an exercise of alchemical transmutation, which I cover in other works.

We as consciousness at one time came from the source, and we have the opportunity to return to it, but with the knowledge of our own existence, which we don't have when we begin. To get that knowledge, we as consciousness have to descend through the dimensions into the matter of the three-dimensional universe.

Everything is modified light, tempered by the laws of a dimension, and in this dimension we have the ability to learn. It's like going to school, but we learn in the school of life through the interaction of darkness and light.

This is why there is so much suffering and opposition to good, as we need opposition in order to learn. Darkness gives form; where there is only light there is no form and there can be no knowledge.

Although we are here to learn, we can also learn badly and not make use of the time we have while we're alive. There is a process of enlightenment, which for consciousness is like the process of creation in reverse. Consciousness when it emerges from the source splits according to the dimensions it exists in, and in enlightenment, all these parts are gathered back and we return to the source as one, awakened and with self-knowledge.

This process is what I do in my life; everyone does something, and I work to gain knowledge and gather back the parts of my consciousness. I'm not specialized in astral projection—it's a tool I use for knowledge in my journey back to the source.

WHAT'S COVERED IN THE BOOK

This book covers the basics of out-of-body experiences (OBEs), the astral plane, and lucid dreaming, in the context of their use for spiritual development. It explains what astral projection is, where we go when we have an OBE, and some of the things you can do when you have one.

Once you get the basics right, you'll be able to go on to get more profound knowledge and experience later, having your feet on a strong foundation, as when it comes to astral experiences, it's easy to get caught on sidetracks and waste time with imagination, rather than having real ones that make a difference to your life.

Many experiences in the astral plane are just fantasy from the imagination, but some are real—I'll show how these imaginary experiences happen and what real ones are.

The most effective way to astral project is through a program, where a set of exercises is practiced over a defined period of time.

I'll also explain about the usefulness of concentrating thought. There are lots of exercises to astral project, but the most essential component to get right is the ability to focus the mind on one thing.

Most astral projection exercises stem from this and use it. There are other techniques such as using sound (mantras), but even they are more successful when you have the ability to concentrate.

I also want to explain a little about dreams, how you can remember them better, and have lucid dreams, which is to realize you're in a dream and wake in the astral plane.

I'll also look into what dreams are, how to understand them, where we are when we have them, what their relationship with out-of-body experiences is, what they mean, how to have clearer and more meaningful dreams, where they come from, and how to use them to understand yourself better and to make significant changes to yourself.

What I won't do in this book is to give techniques to astral project with, as this is a description about the astral dimension and its significance for spiritual development, rather than being a guide to having out-of-body experiences.

If you do successfully have out-of-body experiences though, you'll probably be amazed at what you discover; in fact, the potential for learning is endless.

THE ORIGIN OF THE BOOK

I learnt to astral project in 1990 and taught it for many years. More than ten years after I began teaching, the Internet became more available, and so in 2001 I put together the exercises as a free online course in astral projection, in PDF format. It was later published as a course book and the course stopped running in 2010. The book has now been updated and the course has been removed from it. The questions and my answers at the end of some of the chapters are from that online course.

I've included some of my experiences here from around the first two years of my astral practices, as they illustrate some of the practices I used and things I did to make astral projection work. They may be useful for illustrating the kinds of things you can encounter when you're learning about astral projection. I haven't included anything beyond that as much of it becomes too esoteric and would require a lot of explaining for it to make sense.

MY BACKGROUND IN TEACHING ASTRAL PROJECTION

I've been practicing and teaching astral projection since 1990, and I've used it for my own spiritual and personal development. I learnt in an esoteric school run by a teacher from Colombia called Rabolu, and he learnt from the spiritual teacher Samael Aun Weor. It was their exercises that I mostly used to astral project with. I taught in Rabolu's school between 1990 and 1999, and ran a school between 2000 and 2009 where I taught courses in astral projection to more than ninety thousand people. The astral course I created included exercises I had learned from Rabolu's and Samael Aun Weor's teachings plus my own experience of teaching and practicing astral projection. The course I created had a good success rate; of those who completed it, 67 percent said they had an out-of-body experience while taking it.

This experience has enabled me to give practical solutions to overcome some of the most common difficulties encountered in astral projection. I'm aware of many of the things that work and I've been gradually refining them over time, discovering why some things succeed and others don't.

I've always taught astral projection as part of a larger process of spiritual development, as it is part of a whole and is incomplete without the wider context. Using astral travel to gain spiritual knowledge has enabled me to go to hidden places outside the body and gain access to very esoteric experiences, which have given me a much greater understanding of the workings of the astral world and what's there, than if I were to have simply concentrated upon being an astral traveler.

MY EXPERIENCE OF THE ASTRAL PLANE

I always felt there was something strange about dreams, which was unexplained in science. As a child of around six or seven, I'd have dreams which were so real that I would jump into the air and fly in them; it was the sense of "reality" in them which made me feel that they were a connection to another world.

So many strange things happened in my dreams, but it was the premonitions that gave me information about my life that could only have come from some other "knowing" source that made me feel that something deeper was behind them. I also felt there were extra forces at play, which seemed to come from more than just "me."

As I went into my teens, I remembered dreams less and less. It was as if I was going into deeper sleep than I used to have as a child, and what's more, by the time I was in my early twenties, the only dreams I could recall were nightmares. I felt there had to be reasons for this and I realized that they were due to my own psychological state, which had become numbed and less aware as my teens progressed, and by the time I was in university, my consciousness had dimmed even further.

As I got into my mid-twenties, I decided I'd had enough of living a purely material life—it seemed to lack something indefinable and yet essential. I decided to dedicate my time to searching for spirituality, not as a belief, but through personal experience. I found how I could understand more when I discovered self-knowledge, the knowledge from studying within, and so I practiced it as much as I could.

The more I studied my thoughts, emotions, and actions, and practiced being aware of the present moment, the clearer my dreams became. I also practiced astral projection intensively, and as I progressed, the nature of my dreams changed—there were dreams I could learn from again. I could then study how I acted and felt in them, and I also felt that "other knowing source," which had been giving me information in dreams that I had no other means to obtain, had returned.

My first astral experience happened as a result of an exercise to astral project with a group of people in Rabolu's esoteric school, and a few experiences followed soon after. I wasn't born with the ability to consciously leave my body like some people; I had to learn how to do it, and had to overcome many obstacles, while maintaining it took a great struggle.

Through out-of-body experiences I could see and interact with people who were dreaming. I was also able to meet other people who were having an OBE at the same time and was able to verify that they had been present by checking with them when back in the ordinary world. This showed me that out-of-body experiences were real.

As a couple of years of dedicated practice and disciplined hard work went by, I improved my ability to concentrate and I found that I could consistently leave my body, even being able to go in and out of my body multiple times in a night. When I combined this with the technique to become self-aware while dreaming I was able, after about two years of study, to consistently have an out-of-body experience approximately every other day. In the longer term this amount has varied, often according to my life's circumstances, particularly as concentration is a skill that requires steady practice to maintain and it was not always possible to maintain it.

As time went on, I continued to explore within myself, I used esoteric practices to go into the unknown within myself, and the experiences and knowledge became more spiritual and profound. They are the kinds of things that you would read about in ancient religious texts and see on the walls of ancient sacred sites—some have been wondrous beyond words, while others have been terribly painful. It has helped me to uncover the principles of spiritual enlightenment and to use them in my own life. I have discovered that these principles are contained in ancient religions and that there was once a universal solar religion, which was expressed through different cultures in different ways throughout time. Through my own esoteric experience I've been able to discover the core processes in enlightenment, or the return to the source, the absolute, the great consciousness, or oneness, to give it some of its common descriptions. And in this the ability to learn from the existence beyond this plane has been invaluable.

ASTRAL TRAVEL FOR SPIRITUAL KNOWLEDGE

Many people approach the astral world with a sense of curiosity, or go there for fun, but it's actually another dimension and it should be taken very seriously—other beings exist there. Out-of-body experiences are best taken as a useful tool for a spiritual life, rather than being for fun experiences. This is because they have a context. The astral world is one of the planes in another dimension, and there are other dimensions above it, as well as inferior regions. Only learning about the astral plane is to learn only about a part of a bigger picture, whereas it's better to actually have the bigger picture. Secondly, existence there is "spiritual" in a wider sense. There are other beings over there and what goes on there is part of a spiritual life. There are teachings, spiritual beings, sinister entities, esoteric processes, and many of those that exist there have an awareness of the spiritual processes of life and its higher purpose. To ignore all this would be to go into the astral world with blinders on—it's far better to clear your mind of preconceptions and be open to its learning, and when you do that, you tap into a different way of living.

In my view, the astral plane is best explored by those who want to understand the process of spiritual awakening and practice it fully. There's too much room for the mind to create illusion and fantasy, so that people who are not serious can mix fantasy and reality without being able to distinguish between the two.

I'll refer in this book to higher spiritual beings and also to sinister entities—that's because I know from experience they are there. If you've had experience of them you'll understand, but if you haven't, keep an open mind and don't let it put you off reading the book. If you astral project you'll in the most part be going into the unknown, so if your preconceived ideas and beliefs get in the way, you can easily block yourself from exploring reality. The spiritual is real, but it's nonphysical matter—don't let what you think stop you from understanding it.

If you're looking for a way to connect with spiritual guidance from higher worlds and spiritual beings, to explore the hidden reality and the nature of life beyond the physical world, you'll have a means to do it through astral projection.

OBEs AND LIFE

If you can be clear while you're in the astral plane you'll see life as it is; a life you won't see here. You can potentially discover much about very profound and important things like the purpose of living, and what's the best use you can make of your life.

The physical world is a part of existence, but it's not everything. People are dying every day and leaving the physical world and one day you will too. Dying is a permanent out-of-body experience; to know death while alive means having out-of-body experiences.

Most who have near-death experiences describe a spiritual experience, but not all—some describe hellish ones. It's worth learning about hell while still alive, so that you have learnt how to avoid it before your body is dead.

We are consciousness in matter and we have the ability to transcend matter by traveling out of the body. It is for us to use time and matter wisely, or to squander it. What you do with it is your choice, but you have the ability to leave your body and temporarily transcend physical matter, and learn and discover more about consciousness, enlightenment, life, death, and the multi-dimensional universe, and to put that knowledge to good use.

CHAPTER TWO

OUT-OF-BODY
EXPERIENCES

OUT-OF-BODY EXPERIENCES ARE much more common than most people think. It is estimated that more than 10 percent of the world's population has spontaneously had an out-of-body experience, and this figure rises to over 55 percent if we include lucid dreams, which are actually a kind of OBE. That's a lot of people.

We can find references to OBEs going back far into history, to ancient Egypt, Greece, Tibet, and many other places. In fact most of the world's religions have a belief in other worlds or planes of existence of one kind or another. They are experienced by people all around the world, although their cultural expression may sometimes be different.

THE DIFFERENT KINDS OF OUT-OF-BODY EXPERIENCES

An out-of-body experience occurs when consciousness separates from the physical body, and in a typical experience a person floats up from their body.

Out-of-body experiences usually happen in three ways:

∞ Firstly from dreaming—this is called lucid dreaming. When this happens, we know that we are in a dream and realize that we are out of the body, just as we are aware of being here in this physical world.

∞ Secondly they can occur from consciously leaving the body, usually while it falls asleep—this is commonly known as astral projection. Sometimes these experiences happen spontaneously, but they can be learnt so that they happen voluntarily with the appropriate techniques.

∞ Thirdly they happen with near-death experiences. These are out-of-body experiences that take place with the death of the body. Around 12 percent of those who die and are revived recall having had one.

By having OBEs using the techniques of astral projection and lucid dreaming, we can explore the nature of near-death experiences and get an understanding of death that would be impossible to achieve elsewhere. This is in no way done by inducing death or near-death experiences, but by using the natural connection we have to the astral plane through the normal process of sleep, and should be practiced without stressing, harming, or altering the natural state of the physical body in any way. Attempts to have out-of-body experiences should never be made by attempting to have near-death experiences, as this could prove fatal. The exercises are most effective the more healthy, well rested, and psychologically sound a person is.

Dreams are related to OBEs—they occur in the same place as OBEs, and when we dream we are actually out of the body. We can verify this by having a lucid dream or by projecting and seeing unconscious or partly-conscious dreamers. When we are dreaming however, we don't always see where we are because of the subconscious projections of the mind, so we don't realize what's happening; in an average dream the psyche is locked into the images and model of the world it has unconsciously created, is without self-awareness, and the ability to question the situation.

Dreams can tell us many important things about ourselves and are an indispensable tool for self-discovery. But if you're looking to conventional science to tell you about the function of dreams, you'll probably be disappointed as it doesn't have the means to study their origins. But it is possible to understand them through objective inner exploration, which includes having OBEs as part of a broader study of consciousness.

Because dreams and OBEs are personal experiences, the actual event cannot be seen by current scientific means, nor can science today properly understand them; therefore, the best way to explore dreams is through personal experience. In this way you'll gain your own knowledge about yourself and how you function on a spiritual/psychological level. By doing that you'll also be able to understand the fundamental principles behind astral and dream experiences, including other people's and what the causes are, and you will understand more about the nature of consciousness. This is much more effective than just studying intellectually, which provides lots of theories but little or no experience.

THE ASTRAL PLANE

The most common place we go to when out of the body is called the "astral plane." When we have an out-of-body experience, we are most likely to go to the first of the two planes that constitute the fifth dimension—today this is what is known as the astral plane, although it is not really a scientific term, it's the name that's most widely used today.

If you want to find the closest current scientific theory about the astral plane you could take a look at quantum physics; it's an area of science that's constantly developing. Some theories put forward the existence of parallel universes, and it's been discovered that minute particles behave unpredictably according to laws different to ours. Some suggest that the third and fifth dimensions meet at the molecular level.

Voluntarily projecting to the fifth dimension is a different kind of science though; it's an internal science, rather than a conventional one. It involves personal knowledge gained from experience, experimentation, study, and exploration from within your own psyche.

Being in the astral plane is provable to those who do it, and there have been many cases of people seeing objects, places, or events while out of the body, then later being able to tell others about them, while to observers they were asleep and had no way of knowing about them. It is something real; it's not a figment of the imagination, but another dimension that actually exists.

In an astral experience you are out of your body and you can know it, in the same way that you know you are in the three-dimensional world. It's quite common to see the body left behind when we have an OBE, as the three-dimensional part stays behind. When we astral project, we leave behind everything that is not of the fifth dimension and above. Then what we see when we are there in the fifth dimension is fifth dimensional matter, including the fifth dimensional counterpart of everything in the physical world.

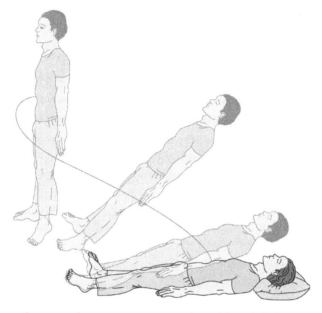

Just as there are laws governing and enabling life here, so too is the astral plane governed by its own laws. But you can do things there that you can't do here, like flying—you can jump into the air and stay airborne, you can fly upward, and then as many people have done, you can fly somewhere you wish to go. Life can look as normal as it does here, but in an OBE you're actually out of your body and know it, in the same way that you know you're in the three-dimensional world.

You actually find yourself in another dimension, existing outside the three-dimensional world. You will be able to go through walls and objects, meet people, travel to distant places in the world and beyond—it's a profound experience.

SOME OF THE BENEFITS OF HAVING OUT-OF-BODY EXPERIENCES

Having OBEs can change your whole view of life. Although you can just astral travel and have some random experiences, it's a huge waste of an opportunity to treat it superficially or like a hobby; it's far better to have the aim to do something fundamentally worthwhile in the astral world.

With this in mind, in an OBE you can meet and receive teachings and guidance from spiritual beings, discover secret knowledge, learn about yourself, and see what and where your spiritual obstacles and inner defects are. You can monitor your spiritual progress knowing each step that you have made, learn about the process of awakening, get premonitions of the future, discover the purpose of your life, discover what happens with death, and much more.

Just by being in the astral plane you can get access to incredible knowledge that is denied to the majority of people in the world. But you can get much more advanced knowledge if you walk along the spiritual path to enlightenment.

You will get more out of astral travel if you consider it not just as a trip to another dimension, but in terms of doing the most effective things possible while you're there. After all, in the span of a human life, time spent consciously in that dimension is limited compared to the amount of time spent in the three-dimensional world, and so it makes sense to make good use of it.

Not surprisingly, you can learn a lot about death from going into the astral plane, because the dead usually go there when initially leaving the body before moving on to other regions or dimensions.

Visions, divine visitations, spiritual beings of all kinds, and apparitions in religions and mythology all have their roots in the higher dimensions. Beings both spiritual and malevolent exist in the fifth dimension, and if you travel enough you will meet both kinds, whether you have a belief about them or not.

Many paranormal phenomena such as hauntings and ghosts are fifth-dimensional, and yet affect the three-dimensional world. The most accurate way to discover their source is to astral project and actually go to the source itself. Paranormal researchers would do well to include astral projection as part of their tool kit.

By traveling out of the body you can see something of what is going on beyond the physical world, and it's better to find this out personally than accepting or rejecting what someone else has said or written.

MY FIRST ASTRAL PROJECTION

The first astral experience I had was with a group of about twelve people doing a practice in Rabolu's esoteric school. It was nighttime and the instructor asked us to go into a different practice room and look at everything in it very intensively. I observed everything in the room in great detail: the ceiling, the walls, and all the objects. We were in silence and I tried to look as clearly as possible without thoughts clouding my perception. When we felt really "there," each of us went back into the other room to lie down and to try to astral project back into the room we had just observed. The teacher had told us that he was going to place an object in that room while we were lying down and he had given us the task to go back there in the astral plane and to see what it was that he had put in it.

As I lay down I tried to keep that awareness, not letting myself be taken away with thoughts. I concentrated on the room intensively, remembering all the little details that I had seen. Soon afterward I began to rise out of my body; everything seemed strange. It was such a new and shocking feeling that I became very frightened and shouted "Help, help," but no one could hear me in the physical world because I was in the astral plane. I looked around and saw that the teacher had also projected. He was sitting there and another man, the spiritual teacher Rabolu, had appeared in the room. He had been drawn into the room by the strength of the exercise. My fear unfortunately brought me back to my body. I looked around and I was surprised that no one had heard me shouting.

Later on I spoke to the teacher and he confirmed that the man whom we both knew had been there. Although it was brief, it was an amazing experience; I had discovered that it was possible to leave the physical body and even meet with people there.

THE DIFFERENT DIMENSIONS

When we have an out-of-body experience, we, the psyche, pass from this dimension into another one. We are multi-dimensional and there are more than just four (length, width, height/depth, time) dimensions. It's at the minute level that they meet; the different dimensions all exist in the here and now and interpenetrate each other without becoming mixed up.

There are seven dimensions in total.

∞ The first three constitute the physical: length, width, and height.

∞ The fourth is time.

∞ The fifth dimension is eternity, which is beyond time. There are two planes in that dimension: the astral and the mental.

∞ The sixth dimension is sometimes known as the causal world. It is the dimension of the soul and it's where consciousness resides.

∞ The seventh dimension is the dimension of the spirit.

Beyond these dimensions is the Absolute, the source, from which the dimensions and all of life spring.

I'm aware of the existence of these higher dimensions because I've been to many of them, and have merged my consciousness with its higher spiritual aspects in the sixth, and seventh dimensions.

The infra-dimensions are inferior zones where most people have gone to when having nightmares. They are accessible through an opening, a portal in space in the astral plane, known in mythology as "the mouth of hell." They are what are referred to as hells in various religions, or the Abyss. I've been to these infra-dimensions very many times whilst out of the body.

This book only deals with going to the astral plane of the fifth dimension; it's the easiest to get to. The infra-dimensions can be accessed from the inferior astral plane, which is where most people go to dream.

The sixth and seventh dimensions are much more difficult to reach than the fifth—to reach the sixth requires not just a concentrated mind, but a silent one too, while the seventh can only be reached by those whose consciousness is already in the dimension of the spirit. In an NDE, the tunnel effect followed by the light that many go through is due to the crossing between the fifth and sixth dimensions; the spiritual realms they are in are usually sixth-dimensional. Most OBEs happen in the astral plane and this is the region I refer to when discussing out-of-body experiences, unless otherwise stated. You can know of these dimensions and planes if you have created the bodies that allow you to exist there, and these bodies are created in the process of enlightenment.

QUESTIONS AND ANSWERS

Is astral travel the same as lucid dreaming?

Astral travel is travel in the astral plane; it includes lucid dreaming and also travel after a conscious projection. When you're astral traveling, you're self-aware in the astral plane of the fifth dimension, knowing you are there.

Can I move objects in the astral environment?

You can move astral objects in the astral environment, just as you can move physical ones here. The astral plane has its own matter, just as the physical world does.

Is it possible to attract the attention of people in the three-dimensional world and interact with them while I move about in my astral travels?

You are extremely unlikely to be able to interact with people who are in the third dimension while you are in the fifth dimension, although you can see the astral part of the person who is in the three-dimensional world, whether they be shopping, etc., because of the interpenetration of the different dimensions in the here and now. But they are different dimensions, so one cannot be directly touched by the other, although they can influence each other. In the three-dimensional world a person may sometimes see or feel things from higher dimensions, such as feeling the presence of a deceased person, but these things are rare.

Is it true that only certain people can astral travel, and that it is the kind of thing you inherit "genetically"?

No, anyone can learn to astral travel. Many people who have traveled had never done it until they learnt how to.

I really want to learn how to do this, but I'm scared that when I do start to split I'll become frightened and won't get to enjoy the experience.

Get more information on it and only try to have an OBE if you feel comfortable and confident in attempting it. Feeling fear is only natural to start with, but you can overcome it as you practice. After you've split from your physical body for the first time, in retrospect you'll probably cherish the experience as something new and magical, and it will have confirmed the reality of the astral world for you. Once you learn more about it and have experienced it more, you'll be able to approach it with more stability, and it will become better and more magical.

I'm very interested in gaining spiritual knowledge through astral travel, but is it also possible to gain knowledge on any other subjects while out traveling, for example, information we can use in daily life?

Yes, you can—the astral plane is just another dimension of life, it's a source of all sorts of knowledge, all of which you could bring back here when you return.

If I astral travel, is my body sleeping and resting so that I will wake up refreshed as always, or will it be tired after I start traveling?

In astral travel the body sleeps just the same as normal. So when you wake up, you feel refreshed just the same, because the fourth-dimensional vital or etheric body charges the physical body up while we sleep.

What's the difference between an out-of-body experience and astral projection?

Out-of-body experiences cover all experiences of being out of the physical body in the astral and higher dimensions and lower planes, while astral projection refers specifically to projecting out of the physical body into the astral plane of the fifth dimension.

When you project, why can you still see things on the material plane?

When you project, you're not seeing actual physical matter, but the astral part of what is in the physical world, because everything that exists here also exists there.

Is there ever any chance I won't be able to get back to my physical body after I've been astral traveling?

No, we are attached to the physical body by a silver cord that always brings us back. We go to the astral world every night when we go to sleep. The only difference with astral traveling is that we are aware of the fact that we're in another dimension instead of dreaming and not being aware of it. In fact, you usually get pulled back to your body too soon; the hard part is staying out there.

What's the difference between lucid dreaming and astral projection?

The difference between lucid dreaming and astral projection is that you project from your body during astral projection, while in lucid dreaming you become conscious that you are in the astral world from a dream. Although in lucid dreaming the dream images can tend to distort what's there more frequently, as long as you're not affected by those, you can do the same things as if you had projected there because you are in the same place.

— Relax the Body

Meditation
- *Remember Obe*
- *See obj. close eyes + recreate it*

CHAPTER THREE

PREPARING FOR ASTRAL PROJECTION

TO MAKE ASTRAL PROJECTION WORK requires using effective techniques; however, it's important to prepare the grounds for projecting into the astral plane, because if you can get the preparation right it will be easier to project and you will be able to go out of your body much more often. Without adequate preparation the techniques to project are less likely to work.

The period of building skills for astral projection is similar to acquiring skills for almost anything. An athlete needs to train in order to race for example, or a builder needs to learn a whole range of things in order to build a house. Rushing into a technique is ineffective. It's like an athlete running a race without training. For an athlete the training develops the technique, physical endurance, strength, etc., that is required to successfully race. I learnt these pre-paratory techniques from the teachings of Rabolu and trained myself in them using his teachings while I was in his esoteric school.

Although out-of-body experiences can happen suddenly and without any preparation whatsoever, preparation is usually required for most people to achieve them on a regular basis.

One of the first things to do is to prepare your environment for astral projection. Try as much as you can to have a quiet sur-rounding where you can be undisturbed. Have a harmonious environment that's not a mess. And, have some quiet time before you begin. It will be more difficult if you go straight from the TV or computer to your astral exercise, than if you prepare with a less fascinating activity and a quiet environment.

The first exercise to learn is to relax and then to learn how to concentrate and visualize. Exercises of concentration and visualiza-tion greatly assist both beginners and those with more experience in the ability to astral project. We'll begin with relaxation.

RELAXATION

It's important to learn to relax the whole body for projection to take place. If you're tense it will be more difficult to focus upon the exercise you're doing and it will be more difficult for the astral and physical bodies to separate and to fall asleep; sleep is needed for astral projection. So an exercise of relaxation prepares you for the astral exercises that will follow.

This is a very simple technique and can be done easily; it's a matter of relaxing all the muscles in the body.

> Lie down on your back with your legs straight and your arms by your side, or if you're sitting, remain in a position you can maintain with the minimum of tension.

Go through each muscle, relaxing them all one by one. You can start anywhere as long as you go through each muscle methodically, making each one completely relaxed.

Pay particular attention to the face once you get to it. There can be little areas of tension that are easily overlooked—relax them all.

Once you have checked everywhere, repeat the procedure—just to make sure that there are no areas of tension that you have missed or that have been reintroduced—and aim to be totally relaxed.

In this state you are now ready to begin your exercise of astral projection.

Practice this every night before you go to sleep and also before you do your concentration exercises. Do this for as long as you feel you need to, in order to prepare yourself for your astral exercises. When you go to do your exercises of projection, you should always relax like this first.

Spend whatever time it takes to relax your muscles, which is normally about five minutes once you learn to do it properly.

Here's a variation on the technique that you could also try. Relax each muscle of the body by tensing each muscle slightly and then immediately letting it go loose. Go through the whole body this way, paying attention to parts of the body that could be tense.

Another part of the preparation is learning to concentrate and visualize. When you feel confident that you can relax your body, you are ready to learn to concentrate and visualize. A relaxation can be done before concentrating and visualizing.

CONCENTRATION

To successfully project it is very important to be able to concentrate on the particular exercise of astral projection you are doing at the time, without being distracted from it by other thoughts or by anything else.

To do that, train yourself to concentrate and visualize for a period of time before you begin your astral exercises and after you have learnt to relax. This need not take long, and you can always continue to develop your concentration exercises after you have begun to try to astral project at night. You don't lose anything by starting the astral projection exercises soon, but just bear in mind, they are less likely to succeed until you improve your ability to concentrate.

> Aim to make concentration exercises part of your daily exercises for astral projection, to keep your mind sharp and focused and more ready for projection.

> Willed astral projection usually occurs when the mind is concentrated at the exact moment that sleep arrives.

> Most techniques for astral projection are variations of concentrating the mind and/or visualizing.

> Being concentrated is having the mind and the whole of one's attention on one thing alone.

It's possible to concentrate upon whatever activity you do at one time. That ability is developed by learning to do one thing at a time in daily life. Sitting exercises of concentration also train and develop the ability to concentrate upon any astral or spiritual exercise.

Being concentrated upon one thing is different from having the mind completely silenced. There are techniques for silencing the mind, but they are not dealt with here because they allow for travel to dimensions above the fifth and are not specific to the subject of astral projection.

You can also get different psychic phenomena occurring when you concentrate. During a concentration practice one time I sat on cushions in front of a candle and had a strange experience where after some time concentrating on the candle, I looked at it in great detail, and with full awareness, but I realized that my eyelids were closed and that I was seeing in a different way, then as soon as I realized this my vision returned to normal, it became dark, and I opened my eyes. At another time when I concentrated on a candle, the concentration was focused just right and I went out of my body straight into the flame, then in a millisecond I was back in my body; there was no sensation of heat from the fire and it was just a quick experience.

After two years of practicing astral projection I was fortunate to live close to the countryside and some small mountains. Having a mountain so close meant that I could concentrate on my practices all weekend without interruption, and on any days or hours I had free during the week, I would go out for walks for hours and just concentrate on what I was doing, trying to be aware all the time, then I would go back home and practice concentration or meditation or astral projection.

This built up a strong level of concentration and frequently I was able to lie down, concentrate on my heart, and leave my body, and as soon as I came back into it I would concentrate on my heart again to leave my body, and when I came back I would just repeat it. At the time I also learnt to go into the astral plane by concentrating on where I wanted to go; it proved pretty effective.

VISUALIZATION

You can also use visualization for astral projection and as a preparation for it. Visualization is using the concentrated mind to consciously imagine or remember something; it has order and structure, unlike the random jumble that much of the free-flowing fantasy kind of imagination has.

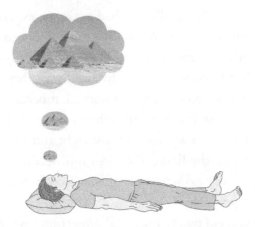

It's possible to actually visualize something that's real, which you know nothing about, if the mind is focused enough—this can be demonstrated in some kinds of remote viewing. The more concentrated and the less in the subconscious and the subjective elements of the psyche you are, the better you can visualize.

No matter how well you visualize, the subconscious will have some kind of effect, but in many successful visualizations the effect of the subconscious is minimized. It doesn't matter necessarily that you get something from your subconscious when you're visualizing for astral projection, as it's the effect of concentrated thought in and of itself that has the biggest impact.

You can train yourself in concentrated thought with something that is entirely from your imagination and isn't actually real, and can project with concentrated thought upon something entirely imaginary. Although what it is you are imagining may have an effect upon what it is you experience in the astral plane, not necessarily, but possibly.

I prefer to use real things in order to minimize the effect of the subconscious upon the astral world, and because it's easier to stop the visualization of something real from becoming fantasy.

DIFFERENCES BETWEEN VISUALIZATION AND FANTASY

There's a difference between this kind of visualization and fantasy, although they are similar. With fantasy the mind goes where it wants to without any continuous direction or sustained concentrated thought, but the "wanting" is usually determined by the subconscious. — *hey sub*

Most of what exists in fantasy is a product of the subconscious, and its random scattered images make it less effective for projection. Moreover, fantasy feeds the subconscious elements of the psyche adding to the general haphazard, scattered mind during the day and adding to the likelihood of having vague and weird types of dreams without meaningfulness in them.

PRACTICING SITTING CONCENTRATION AND VISUALIZATION

The more the mind is trained to concentrate and visualize, the better it becomes at it. It's a matter of practice.

That's why it helps to carry out exercises of concentration and visualization and why they are given as a preparation for projection.

As you learn astral projection, you will benefit a great deal in your ability to project if you train yourself daily in concentration and visualization.

If you train daily your chances of projecting will be dramatically increased. It's like an athlete who prepares for a race by training.

To train the mind to concentrate and visualize, do exercises where you sit or lie down simply to concentrate and/or visualize.

It's important not to force the mind. Start with small amounts of concentration and visualization, say five or ten minutes, and gradually build up to a level that you are comfortable with, for example, twenty minutes.

When you go to do your exercise to actually project then the mind is already trained to concentrate and visualize and the projection is more likely to succeed.

When trying to practice concentration and visualization or when trying to astral project, one of the main obstacles is the continuously chattering, daydreaming mind.

Practice the concentration/visualization exercises daily to prepare for projection and then maintain them daily whenever you want to astral project.

THE PROBLEM OF CHATTERING THOUGHTS

Attempts at astral projection usually fail because the mind is unable to be concentrated on one thing. It's used to chattering away all day, or being fascinated with whatever activity is taking place, so when you try to do an exercise to project, the mind carries on chattering. Thoughts that were so active during the day continue to be active and they interrupt the exercise, causing the astral projection attempt to fail.

However, when you are aware and concentrated upon whatever activity you are doing in a given moment in daily life, you train and educate the mind to be focused upon one thing and cut down the chatter and interfering inner states (egos), so that when you do your exercise of projection you have a more focused mind and are more able to concentrate upon the exercise, making it more likely to succeed.

A series of exercises that can be done throughout the day can be created and built into a program lasting days or weeks. This helps us to carry out one activity at a time and focus more upon whatever it is we're doing, without thinking about lots of other things at the same time.

It's of course necessary to use the mind to be able to think and plan, remember things, solve problems, create/invent things, carry out tasks, etc., but the problem is that its activity is so compulsive—it just runs of its own accord, and it's difficult for it to be on one thing and be profoundly concentrated for any period of time. The mind is scattered and the thoughts go on and on, like a wheel turning around and around. Ultimately, if someone creates the inner bodies with alchemy (refer to other works of mine for a description of what I mean by alchemy), they can be in peace and use the mind as a tool.

When the mind is trained to concentrate, it's possible to direct it at will to a psychic task such as astral projection or meditation and be successful in it.

The ability to focus the mind is not something that happens overnight, although it is possible to get it right occasionally in the beginning. It takes time to gradually educate the mind to be concentrated on just one thing, as it is not used to functioning like that. It requires a great deal of practice to train the mind to focus, but you can start right away with it and it will benefit everything that follows.

If you are not concentrated when trying to project, you will either get taken into sleep by a thought, or will become restless and unable to sleep. Either way, being able to concentrate fixes the problem.

Being able to properly concentrate and visualize is the way to be able to project at will, whenever we want to, as long as there are no other factors such as illness that can stop us. In one night it is possible to project many times, going out into the astral plane, coming back, going back out again, and so on.

Although it is rare, it is actually possible to astral project with the eyes open. For example, as I've discovered while concentrating upon an object and looking at it, the concentration can be so intense that with the eyes open one can go straight out of the body and into the object.

It could be said that in this case the projection took place while I was awake, but in fact, even though my physical body had signs of being awake, I was actually sleeping in certain ways. Even though it may not be normal sleep, concentration can bring about the processes that take place with sleep that result in projection, even though other what we would call normal signs of sleep, such as closed eyes, etc., may not be present.

The concentration and visualization exercises given in this book are not the only ones that work. The essential element in astral projection exercises is concentration, and there are many variations of concentration and visualization. Most variations of visualization or concentration will work as techniques for projection, which is why it is so important to develop these skills at an early stage.

With the ability to concentrate, all the techniques of astral projection work. Even sound and mantras require a degree of concentration to be successful.

EXERCISES OF CONCENTRATION AND VISUALIZATION

I've divided concentration and visualization exercises into two types—those done on an object or a place, and those using imagination. Each of them has a particular purpose. They should initially only be tried for a very short period of time, such as five to ten minutes, and you can increase them gradually depending upon what you feel you need.

CONCENTRATION AND VISUALIZATION ON AN OBJECT

This is a technique to visualize the details of an object and remember it. It's useful training for increasing the ability to concentrate and visualize in the exercises for astral projection.

To practice it, first pick an object to use—it can be any object (a popular one for this exercise is a lit candle, but make sure that you only use a candle if it is safe to do so and there's no risk of starting a fire). Sit down and place it where you can see it clearly. Then concentrate upon it in great detail, observing how it looks, perceiving its textures, shapes, colors, the material it is made of, the way that light reflects on it, etc., observing whatever you can about it.

When you've clearly observed it, then close your eyes and recreate the object in your mind, exactly as you've seen it. If there are things that you can't recreate because you didn't look at them properly, or if the image is fading away, open your eyes and look at it again. Study it, then close your eyes and recreate the image again in your mind. Keep doing this process to visualize it as clearly as you can.

This type of exercise gently trains the mind in concentration and visualization, both of which are vital for astral projection. Try to do it regularly (at least once a day for five to ten minutes) at a different time from your astral projection exercise and whenever is convenient for you, but don't do it for more than ten minutes initially. If you want to do it more times each day then do so, but increase it very gradually, because the mind needs to be educated and trained and shouldn't be forced.

Also, try varying the object you do the exercise with—for example, you could try a glass of water, a plant, flowers, etc., and after the initial attempts, continue with at least ten minutes each day. Remember to close your eyes when you are recreating the object in your mind and to recreate it often. Don't try to stay there with your eyes open or force yourself to keep staring at the object for a long period of time. Gradually increase the time you spend on this exercise, beginning with just a little.

CONCENTRATION AND VISUALIZATION ON AN OBJECT WITH IMAGINATION

This is an extension of the first technique. Take an object—again, it can be any object—and sit down in a place where you can see it clearly. Then concentrate upon it in great detail using the first technique, observing how it looks, seeing its textures, shapes, colors, the material it is made of, the way that light reflects on it, etc., discovering everything you can about it. When you've clearly seen it, then close your eyes and recreate the object exactly as it is in your mind. If there are things that you cannot visualize because you didn't look at them properly, or if the image is fading away, open your eyes and look at it again. Study it, then close your eyes and visualize the image again in your mind. Keep doing this process so that you visualize it as clearly as you can.

When you have clearly visualized the object (while having your eyes still closed), imagine, perceive, and visualize the inside of the object. In the case of a candle for example, go inside the flame and visualize the inside of the flame.

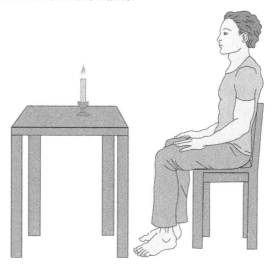

Go further exploring anything else you would like to explore about the object. As you are visualizing/concentrating on it, feel yourself being the object, what it feels like being a flame burning on the tip of a wick. At that point you could ask questions to explore the object, such as: What is fire made of? How does it work? What is it for? What is it to be the object? If you pursue the answers far enough, you may go beyond what the logical mind can find the answers to, into meditation, into the silence of the mind, rather than just being concentrated.

You can learn to focus the mind very well through this simple, but powerful technique. On the surface it looks mundane, but it can be quite a spiritual exercise.

You can do this type of visualization on any object. You could do· it with a pen, a plant, with a flower in a vase on your coffee table in your living room, a glass of water, and so on.

Vary the objects and continue with at least ten minutes each day. You can also try this imaginative visualization/concentration exercise in a quiet and safe spot in nature and on a tree, a rock, an ocean, a lake, or a river, to mention a few. You can also visualize a place by being there or by looking at a photograph or video of it.

IMAGINATIVE VISUALIZATION

This technique is a visualization of something you can't physically see.

Instead of looking at an object or even a photograph, close your eyes and visualize an object or a place at a distance, creating it solely from your imagination or memory, with the aim of seeing it in detail as though it were real, or creating the experience of being there.

Objects or places could be recreated from memories where you try to remember the past as clearly as you can, or be purely imaginary.

Keep to the same time as the other exercises.

TO RECAP:

∞ Learn to relax your body—it takes a short time to learn to relax—and then train yourself to concentrate to prepare yourself for astral projection.

∞ Start with short daily exercises of concentration lasting five to ten minutes, and gradually increase the amount of time to twenty to thirty minutes as you feel comfortable with it.

∞ Relax the body before doing a concentration exercise.

∞ Begin your exercises of astral projection whenever you are ready, but maintain daily concentration exercises whenever you are doing nightly astral projection ones.

MY EARLY ASTRAL PROJECTION ATTEMPTS

After I had my first success at astral projection in the group, which I described earlier, I began to try astral projection at home. I had more success initially in the afternoons where I had an opportunity to lie down and practice.

One afternoon I lay down on my bed on my back, relaxed my body, and began to concentrate on my heartbeat. As I concentrated on it, I felt as though I began to move with the beats of the heart. I was amazed to find that it kept getting stronger and stronger, and I lifted more and more with each beat. A tingling sensation went through my body along with a high-pitched noise until finally I was raised completely out of my body.

I wasn't afraid this time and I calmly looked around the room— it was exactly as it had been in the physical world, with the only difference being that colors and everything looked more intense and that I was hovering above my body. A thought came to me that people say it's possible to create your own reality when in the astral plane. I wondered how this worked and how real it would be, so I imagined a pink toothbrush—to my surprise, it appeared there in the room like a real object. I moved around a bit, looked around to see if it would be gone, but it was still there, as bright and as real as everything else. I wondered what else I could imagine and I started thinking, but began to move downward and merge back into my body, until waking up back into the physical world.

A day or two later I lay down to try to project by concentrating on my heartbeat, which has been the most successful technique for me, only this time as soon as I tried to relax the tingling sensations began and I lifted up out of my body; this time it seemed to be almost involuntary. It was the same process of lifting out as previously, but as I looked around, to my great surprise I was in my room, but the room was exactly as it had been when I was a boy in the 1960s. I was a bit dumbfounded by this, and then I heard the sound of the front door of the house opening and my parents coming in. My mother called my name and started to come up the stairs—her voice sounded younger, I was startled, and I merged back into my body. This was a projection into the akashic records of nature, where everything from the past is recorded; when I opened my eyes in the physical world, my parents had not yet come into the house.

A few days later in another afternoon, I had another OBE. This time I was feeling down about an inner state that I was trying to understand and overcome, but couldn't. I lay down feeling a sense of defeat, even desperation, and almost as soon as my head hit the pillow I was lifted up into the air accompanied by the OBE sensations. This time I got up, sat on the edge of the bed, and looked in the mirror. The astral plane had its luminosity and I looked at myself in the mirror—the reflection that came back was me, but with changes due to the inner state I was trying to understand. It showed in symbolism how that state affected me, but it showed it in a profound way, a way that I could never have grasped here.

Although it's the out-of-body experiences that usually stand out the most in an account like this, it was actually self-knowledge that I put the most effort into, observing myself during the day, being aware, and analyzing the different inner states I'd had to get more knowledge of them. I loved how I could change and see all the things that had trapped me for so long and held me back in so many different ways. At that time I had only recently discovered self-knowledge and learnt how to observe inner states, and I finally had ways to begin to be free of them and to be aware in the present moment. It felt wonderful when my consciousness, through sustained attempts at inner observation and stillness, would be aware and in silence, perceiving the present moment, watching the thoughts, and breaking out of them.

CHAPTER FOUR

THE PROCESS OF ASTRAL PROJECTION

EVERY TIME SOMEONE GOES TO SLEEP, they (the psyche) leave the physical body behind and go into the astral plane of the fifth dimension. This normally takes place unconsciously, but with astral projection we are simply aware of that process taking place.

To astral project we normally need sleep, because it's with sleep that the astral body separates from the physical one. The two bodies are attached by a silver cord that stretches infinitely. It sends messages between one body and the other, which enables the person in the astral body to go back to the physical body as soon as they wake up from sleep. It's this connection which allows a person in the astral plane to unconsciously influence the physical body while dreaming. For example, a person who dreams they are running can unconsciously move their physical arms and legs and an onlooker can see they are trying to run in their dreams. Likewise, the physical body can influence dreams while asleep. If you stroke someone's hand while they are asleep, they may dream that someone is stroking their hand, etc.

If you've ever had a sensation of falling just as you are going to sleep, what you've been aware of is the astral body going back into the physical one. However when this happens you have fallen asleep unconsciously and are not aware of splitting into the astral plane, just the moment of going back into your body. The normal process of projecting and coming back to the body is not as alarming as this because you are not caught by such a surprise.

When we carry out an astral projection technique it causes us to go through the process of sleep consciously. We are then aware of all or some of the processes that take place within the transition period between wakefulness and sleep, until the two bodies separate.

EXERCISES TO ASTRAL PROJECT WITH

There are many exercises for astral projection; the main types I've used are concentration, visualization, and mantras, most of which I learnt when I was in Rabolu's esoteric school. Astral projection exercises have been used successfully by many people over the years, and some are likely to have been used for thousands of years.

I haven't included any exercises of astral projection here as I don't want to box in creativity by restricting them to a specific and limited number or type.

Many people like to have the freedom to try different techniques to stop the exercises from becoming stale. Exploring and examining what works best will accelerate discovery and allow experiences to happen. But whatever exercises you choose, make sure they are safe to do.

With whatever exercises and programs you do use however, to astral project the first thing you need to do is to get into a position in which you can sleep, lying down in bed for example. That's because we detach from the physical body with sleep. For most people, the most effective position for astral projection is to lie down on their back.

Then you need to be able to relax your body because tension will hold you into it. Then, without moving, go straight from the relaxation to your technique for astral projection.

THE PROCESS OF SPLITTING FROM THE BODY

There are a number of different things, sensations, etc., that happen as sleep appears and we leave the body. As you practice astral projection you may feel all of them, some of them, or none of them, in which case, you may just find yourself in the astral plane without being aware of projecting there.

After relaxing, the body may become very heavy, yet at the same time strangely you may feel very light. As you do a technique for astral projection you may find a small very high-pitched noise whirring like a motor inside your head, a feeling of not being able to move, and then a kind of electric sensation passing through the body. As this happens you may feel yourself rising up, lifting up out of the body. As you lift, you have projected—you're in the astral plane.

The sensations of projecting can sometimes be different to the way I've just described. For example, when concentrating on a technique the heartbeats may seem to intensify, and as they get stronger, there is a feeling of moving with them. The sensation increases as we go higher and higher with each beat, until we rise up out of the body.

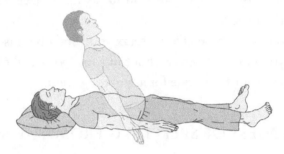

Sometimes during an exercise there may be a feeling of immobilization. This is because the two bodies are separating and the voluntary movement of the physical body is being changed for voluntary movement of the astral body, which happens as we leave the third dimension and go into the fifth. If the exercise is continued however, the immobilization may cease and the astral split occur.

STEPPING OUT INTO ANOTHER DIMENSION

Once we project, we are then in a completely different dimension. If the astral body has projected just a little way out, by lifting up just slightly into the air for example, there may be confusion as to whether an astral split has actually happened. It's possible to check whether astral projection has occurred by looking for differences to the physical world by looking around at the place we're in, whether the room is exactly like it is normally, or if there's anything strange.

Another way of checking is to jump a little in the air and try to fly. If it's the astral plane we can fly and a whole new dimension is open to us to explore—don't try jumping out of the window or anywhere that's unsafe. Always use safe methods to check whether you are in the astral plane. Don't do anything there that you wouldn't consider to be safe here, nor attempt to astral travel without making sure that you're safe and not stressed.

If you have projected higher out of your body, then you know that you're in the astral plane, so there are many possibilities open to you. You may wish to explore by walking outside your house and taking off from the ground and flying (but don't jump from a height), or by traveling to a place you want to go to. If you want to travel somewhere specific, you could just fly there, or you could visualize where you want to go and then go there instantaneously, or you could ask a spiritual being or your own Being to take you somewhere (refer to my other works for more information on the inner Being and spiritual beings). Sometimes though, what you project straight into is what you need to learn from.

As I explained earlier, I found my first experience a bit frightening, going into the unknown, not knowing if I would ever come back. But experience has taught me not to worry. We dream every night; we are in the astral world but nothing bad ever happens to the physical body. We don't get stuck out there because we have a silver cord that attaches us in the astral body to the physical body. It stretches infinitely long (although there is a limit to how far we can go in the universe, determined by other factors) and is never broken unless we die, which doesn't happen by projecting—it doesn't just snap, nor can we get out and not be able to find our way back. The silver cord always pulls us back. We only have to move during sleep or wake up and we're back in the body.

The difficulty is staying out there long enough. It is so easy to get pulled back. When that happens, you usually begin to fade away, or travel backward at a rapid pace until you fall back into the body, or you just feel yourself merging back with the physical body and you wake up physically.

It can help to hold onto an object so that you are not pulled back so quickly while you are there. It's also important to watch that there are no large emotions such as fear or elation at being there, because these can be enough to pull you back straightaway. You also need to be as aware as possible and to maintain that awareness for as long as you can, because any daydreams you have there actually turn into dreams, and before you know it, you're in a dream and you don't realize that you projected until you wake up from sleep.

There's a lot to explain about what you will find in the astral world besides seeing the things that are also here in the physical world, but it's best to use that dimension for your own personal development and spiritual search. Also note that there are other beings in the astral plane besides humans; there are spiritual beings who have awakened in light, and sometimes malevolent beings who have awakened in darkness. I discuss these further in other works of mine and some of the following chapters in the book.

QUESTIONS AND ANSWERS

Are factors like noise (young kids), position of sleep, sharing a bed, and age linked to your ability to astral travel?

Noise and sharing a bed can be a distraction, but if there's no alternative you have to get used to it and concentrate so that you don't notice it. The position of sleep you practice in is the one that you find works best or is practical, but lying on the back works best for most people. Age makes no real difference, but children are less burdened by their subconscious (egos) than adults. As a person becomes more involved and caught up with life, they become more psychologically asleep; however, this can be reversed with the right exercises and spiritual work in general, and then the ability to astral travel can be increased beyond what it was in childhood.

When you astral project, how conscious are you of the experience? Would astral projecting be as conscious as being in the physical body?

Yes, it can be. When you consciously astral project you are conscious of the experience, just as much as being in the physical body. There can also be times when it's a bit dreamlike, but these are exceptions.

What's the reason for the loud sounds which resemble the sound of a bird flying and strange sensations to be felt on the body?

There are symptoms, such as a noise when separation takes place between the bodies, or when the various elements of the subconscious detach and enter the fifth dimension. These are fifth dimensional— we become aware of them as we go into that dimension.

When is the best time to astral project?

We can project at any time—we just need to sleep. Many people have great success with an afternoon nap, particularly when they are not too tired when they try. The night has its own advantages though; the atmosphere is quieter and more conducive to mystical things.

Can reduced daily eating help out-of-body experiences?

Some people say that they find OBEs easier when they eat lightly; however, the main problem people have with astral projection is that there is a lack of concentration. What's needed for astral projection is concentration and sleep, so how much is eaten shouldn't have a huge effect. Having said that, it is not so good to try an astral exercise or go to bed after a very heavy meal because it tends to subtly upset the stomach and that can take you into lower parts of the fifth dimension. On the other hand, there's a need to be careful with fasting because it can cause other problems.

I've found that when I do any of the concentration practices in order to project, after a while I get absolutely freezing feet! I never experience cold feet at any other time, except when I am practicing these astral exercises and the longer I do the exercise for, the colder they get. It has got to the point where I have to wear ski socks every time I do a practice and my feet are still cold! Has anyone else experienced this? Do you know why this might be?

Yes, the body gets colder as we fall asleep. We normally don't notice it, but if we try to astral project, we go much further into the process of sleep and are aware of the increasing cold. Some may be more affected than others.

After starting to travel, will you be able to return to normal sleep?

Yes, normal sleep returns naturally as OBEs generally take efforts to achieve and sustain. Once you start to astral travel, you need to keep doing the exercises to keep going there; otherwise, very little usually happens and sleep goes back to normal. At the end of traveling you'll find you'll usually go back to your body and wake straight up in it, or the astral experience turns into a dream and you wake up the next morning and remember that you've astral traveled.

CHAPTER FIVE

CHECKING WHETHER OUT-OF-BODY EXPERIENCES ARE REAL   *Vish*

ONE OF THE FIRST THINGS you might want to do is to find out for yourself if out-of-body experiences (OBEs) are real. So set yourself some kind of test to find out.

Astral projection experiences tend to be less clear and less objective than near-death experiences (NDEs), but if you understand a few things you can have astral experiences that are just as clear and real as NDEs.

Astral experiences can sometimes be subjective in the way that dreams can be, so even though we are out of the body, we may not accurately perceive reality. What's experienced could be clear, wholly subjective, or a mixture of both, and by understanding how the subconscious works and affects perception you can learn to have clear OBEs.

This depends upon having clear information about the nature of experiences out of the body and also about psychology. It's really important to learn to understand how the mind and emotions work and to use techniques to study yourself.

In surveys in the online course in dreams and out-of-body experiences I used to run, 78 percent said that something told them that what they experienced was real and not a projection from their own mind. If you go into the astral plane, check it and see for yourself.

In a clear OBE it is possible to see not only the reality of that dimension, but also actual objects and events taking place in this three-dimensional (physical) world, as the fifth dimension is also in the here and now. Near-death experiences are also out-of-body experiences. Indeed both kinds of experiences, NDEs and OBEs occur in exactly the same place and the out-of-body traveler can meet the deceased, just as they can meet other living people.

THE SUBCONSCIOUS GETS IN THE WAY

A great problem with the accuracy of OBE and dream experiences is the influence of the subconscious. Many experiences are just projections of the mind and are not real, giving some people the fuel to fire the claim that all OBEs are just subjective, even hallucinatory experiences. Many are, but if you get enough experience and look at some of the accounts of the experiences other people have had, it'll become apparent that not all are.

With the right techniques you can be able to study your own psyche and even change it enough so that you can see and experience real events and places while out of the body.

If subconscious states that exist during daily life are cleared and don't get in the way of what you see, the psyche can become more objective in daily life and, as the psyche is what we take with us when we have an OBE, the out-of-body experiences themselves also become more objective.

If you try to look for information on what's in the astral world to get some idea of what to find there, you'll find all kinds of bizarre, sometimes even contradictory accounts. It's very easy to be misled by the projections of the mind and to be lost in things that are read or heard from others, which may be no more than projections of their subconscious and imagination. Anyone can write virtually anything about the worlds out of the body and they may seem believable, but it can be based solely on the projections of their subconscious, and can even generate a collective subjective and illusory reality. This is why it's important to study the subconscious and learn how to be aware objectively.

THE MISTAKE OF TRYING TO "CREATE YOUR OWN REALITY"

A lot of people want to create their own experience when out of the body by imagining something. You could do that, and if you were to imagine something it would look real there, but that's a waste of an opportunity because you'll be missing what's really there. In one of the first times I projected I experimented after I'd come out of my body; I lifted up and was floating just up from the bed, and I wanted to see if what I'd heard about "creating our own experience" while there was true. Hovering above my bed, my room looked normal, everything was just the same as it was in the physical world, so I had an idea to imagine something to see whether it would become real or not, and if it did, in what sense would it be real.

As I mentioned earlier in the book, I imagined a pink toothbrush, and one appeared in the room right in front of me—it stayed there with a hologram-like quality to it. I wondered whether it would disappear if I thought of something else, but it didn't; it was just like any other object in the room, fixed and immovable. I realized then how powerful the subconscious was in creating a false reality out of the body, and how much I would need to understand this if I was to be able to know and see what was really going on in the astral plane.

In later experiments I looked for evidence of things out of the body, such as objects that I hadn't seen in the physical world, which I could then check and verify the existence of when I was back in my body. One example of this was when I stayed at a country house with a group of people interested in esoteric knowledge; at night we tried a meditation exercise and I projected into the astral plane. I lifted straight up from my body still lying horizontally until I was close to the ceiling. I could see small marks on it, which I hadn't seen before as they were too small to see from the ground. I decided to look at them closely to see if they would be visible when I got back to my body. The next morning I stood on the bed and checked—the marks were identical to what I'd seen out of my body. On other occasions I met other people when having OBEs and saw many other different things that convinced me that real objects, places, and events, can be seen over there.

When we see things in the astral world that look the same as those here, what we're seeing is the astral counterpart of the physical object, since we are actually in the same place, but in another dimension. Whatever is in the third dimension is also in the fifth. So if you've projected into your bedroom at night for example, you could potentially see it as it is in everyday life. You can get up, walk out of your room, go outside, see the place, the town, or city where you live, the outside of your home, the street, etc., all as they are in daily life.

Things don't always look the same though. Something may be different in the bedroom, you might project to a different place, or strange things could be going on. That's because the mind can be projecting something so you won't see it as it is, or on the other hand, there could actually be different things there, or what you see can be created there by higher beings to teach you.

By looking into your psychology and learning how the psyche becomes more objective, you'll become more aware of the nature of what it is that you're experiencing and will be more able to discriminate between the different kinds of experiences you encounter while outside the body.

SOME IDEAS FOR CHECKING THE REALITY OF ASTRAL EXPERIENCES

Here are some examples of how to check at a personal level whether an out-of-body experience is real or not; it's not an exhaustive list, just ones I've used and found to work:

∞ By seeing objects, places, or other phenomena while over there that you have no knowledge of here and then checking them back here. You can carry out tests (if you feel the need to) to check all kinds of objects.

∞ By seeing events while you're out of the body and checking what you've seen when you're back in the physical world.

∞ By getting information about the future and seeing it come true.

∞ By the lucidity of the experience itself, which is something you would have to experience to really make a judgment about.

∞ By meeting with others over there that are also having OBEs and verifying the meeting back here. If you meet someone while having a clear OBE you can relate the experience to each other while back in the physical world.

∞ By experiencing things you had no knowledge of and reading about them later in ancient books, sacred texts, myths and legends, etc.

When you do get astral experiences, you can use the information you get there as a guide—some things are symbolic and need interpreting while others can carry a great deal of importance, so it pays to be very attentive toward them.

By having objective out-of-body experiences you can get in touch with the spiritual aspect of life, which has been lost to most of humanity as it becomes increasingly mechanized and entrapped.

You might find that even though you verify that experiences in the astral plane are real, you have a hard time convincing other people they are, but that's just the way things are. Although out-of-body experiences are fairly common and a real and very natural part of life, they are usually misunderstood, even by the person who has them, let alone by friends, family, doctors, scientists, etc. This is in no small part due to the inability of science to understand and explain them, but it's also due to the nature of the kinds of experiences that occur there and to certain cultural and social restrictions. In the past they have been regarded as a means to receive spiritual and other-worldly experience and communication.

By learning to have conscious and clear OBEs, you can understand what they are and explore deep into the mysteries of life and death, and even if no one else cares, it really doesn't matter—it's what you know and do that counts.

QUESTIONS AND ANSWERS

If you went to the astral plane and saw something like a building that only existed in the astral world, and you described it to me and then I went to look at it, would I see the same thing as you or is the building represented to us based on our own individual experiences and thoughts?

It is possible that it will look the same to us both if it's a real place, but it's also possible that it would be something that's unique to you that's part of your own learning, in which case another person wouldn't see it. Different people can see the same thing in the astral plane because things actually exist in the astral world and all see what's really there. But things can also be put there by higher beings just for one time, for a teaching for example, or they could just be projections of the subconscious mind, in which case they wouldn't be actual items, and would be unlikely to be seen by others. That's one of the reasons why if you want to have clear and objective astral experiences, it's so important to learn about the psyche and be as free as possible of the subjective projections of the subconscious.

As my family lives far away and say for example I get the feeling that my sister is unhappy or in trouble and I want to check on her, if I become adept at astral travel, can I travel in my astral body to where my sister is located in her physical body, unaware of me, and check that she is alright? In other words, can the astral body travel through the physical world and, although it is obviously removed from it, still view the physical world as it exists in physical reality? Or is everything you would experience in the astral body necessarily "false," that is, if I told myself I wanted to go see my sister and suddenly I was there next to her, asleep or whatever, is that my real sister in her real bedroom at home in the real world or is it just a dream "vision" of my sister? I'm just wondering because sometimes I worry about her so much and would like to check on her in this way, but if it is "false"' and just a dream then what is the point?

You can travel in your astral body to see your real sister if you are consciously in the astral plane and your psyche and therefore your perception is not being altered by your subconscious. You will then see the astral counterpart of her physical body. She will be unaware of you unless she is consciously traveling too, but she may remember seeing you in her dreams if she is asleep herself.

Everything that exists in the physical world also exists in the astral world, so if you throw a shoe on the roof of your house in this world, you can go and see where it landed in the astral plane, and then you can find it where you saw it in the astral plane if you go and check it later in the physical world.

Now another question that kind of follows from this one. Say I go visit my sister and she wakes up while I'm there, will she see me? Is the astral body visible to those not in the astral plane? Or will she maybe "feel" my presence on some other, non-visual, intuitive level? If I speak to her, will she hear me, or will my voice enter her mind as thoughts?

It's unlikely that she will see, hear, or feel you. Things are taking place in the astral world all the time and they are not normally perceived here.

That's not to say it can't happen though, because there are latent psychic faculties that could allow it to. These may be increased with exercises to develop psychic faculties, but normally she wouldn't perceive anything.

I'm just beginning to do the exercises and I'm looking forward to astral traveling (hopefully). I'm curious whether I can go to a place that I want to in the real world when I astral travel. Say if I want to go to an exact place at an exact time, is it possible?

You can travel to any place in the three-dimensional world but you will see its astral counterpart, not the three-dimensional one, because you're in a different dimension and see the things that are there. The dimensions intermingle and everything that is in the three-dimensional world has an astral counterpart.

I just wondered if it was possible to meet with other human beings while astral traveling, either while they are astral traveling too or while they are awake and their friend has come to see them by astral travel?

Yes, you can meet with other human beings while astral traveling, but to talk to them meaningfully they also have to be conscious in the astral. Otherwise, if you find them and they are dreaming they may look like drunken people. They are unlikely to recognize you although they may remember seeing you in a dream. You can see people who are awake in the three-dimensional world because you can see their astral counterpart, but you can't communicate with them because they won't normally be able to see you.

CHAPTER SIX

ASTRAL TRAVEL

TRAVEL IN THE ASTRAL PLANE takes a spirit of investigation to be successful in the long run. To be able to do much when you're there, you'd have to learn to get around—it's another dimension and it has different laws. It's natural to want to have profound experiences every time you have an OBE, but it doesn't usually work out like that. You've got to learn how to travel, how to see, maneuver, and discover what kind of things are there.

The mind can be a big stumbling block as it's easy to get confused, so use your intuition more and be less rigid in your ideas and expectations. Explore your way around. It's another dimension of here, so if you are stuck and don't know what to do, a suggestion is to travel somewhere you know exists—this will teach you how to get around.

You can also ask for help to be taken to different places or shown things, but be open to what you see, and don't rely upon divine beings to assist you all the time—you should learn to travel yourself, otherwise you can become passive and lost. Investigate, experiment, and explore actively with intuition and an open mind, without letting sinister forces or your own emotions stop you.

THE SOUL LEAVING THE BODY, BY LUIGI SCHIAVONETTI, 1808.

If you want to explore your psychology, it helps to be able to see the ego states in their individual form. You can do this most effectively in the mental plane, which is a higher plane of the fifth dimension. To get into the mental plane while you are in the astral world, jump upward and backward at the same time and say "Astral body come out of me." If it works, you see your astral body and you'll be in the mental plane, where you'll be able to explore your egos.

It's easy to waste an opportunity to learn something important when you go to the astral world. Time spent flying around nowhere in particular, looking at details on walls, imagining things, etc., is not the best way to use an astral experience. It is better to get esoteric experiences. These may sound unreal at first, but keep an open mind and gain experience. Be prepared for what you find, because existence in other dimensions is different to the physical world. I do explain a little of astral traveling with different beings, but don't let existing attitudes about this put you off. Look at the accounts of people's near-death experiences and get your own astral ones; spiritual beings are real.

I can only give a limited number of examples of what can be done in the astral plane, but it's up to you to discover things for yourself and get your own personal knowledge. Sometimes you'll get esoteric experiences and be taught by spiritual beings when you astral travel, whether you're expecting it or not. Sometimes you may wake up in the astral plane in a situation that's full of symbolic meanings. At other times, however, you may have to seek out the learning.

You can travel to a place by visualizing and concentrating upon where you want to go to, or upon a person or spiritual being you want to see. You can also follow your intuition or ask for spiritual help such as asking your Being (either the male or female aspects of the Being referred to as the Mother or Father) to take you where you need to go. Then either of them can take you somewhere.

Or you can go to a temple or spiritual place to be taught. If you know one, concentrate upon it or ask your divine Being to take you to there to be taught. Don't be surprised if you are not allowed in though, because they require the fulfillment of certain standards to get into many of them, and some standards are very difficult to meet.

TRAVELING TO DIFFERENT PLACES IN THE ASTRAL PLANE

There are different ways to travel somewhere in the astral plane and using your intuition at the time is a good guide. You can always walk in the astral plane, but it's much quicker to fly. You can be taken somewhere if you ask, or you can concentrate upon a specific place and go there immediately, or travel from the spot you are in using what you see there to guide you. If you want to go back to a place you have been to before, visualize it and you can go there.

It's possible to concentrate upon a place and project there directly, or as you go to sleep, you may see dream images. If you concentrate upon one of them, going into it with your visualization, you can go directly into it and be there consciously in the astral world, or you can go back there in a dream and continue your experience.

If you are already in a place in which you are being taught, it's usually better to stay there and continue learning unless it is time to go, or you feel that you should.

Don't worry about getting stuck in the astral plane. We always come back unless the physical body dies: you just wake up from sleep, or more often, straight away after the experience. The difficulty is staying in the astral world without going back to the body. It helps to hold onto something there to stay aware, which will help prevent the conscious experience from becoming a dream, and to watch your emotions, since any emotion can bring you back quickly. Emotions such as fear and worry are major culprits.

When I first learnt to astral travel, I often found that I couldn't sustain myself there—I would fly back to my body quickly, and so I held onto objects there and often moved around securing myself by holding on to whatever I could find of astral matter.

Many times when coming back to my body involuntarily I would either merge into my physical body, firstly being aware of being slightly higher than it, then feeling myself going into it, merging with it and waking up. Very often I would be aware of flying backward at great speed; it was as though everything became a vortex and I was drawn backward into my body, where of course I woke up.

Sometimes in the astral world a being can appear in front of you, sometimes telling you different things. Through intuition you can tell if that being is good or malevolent just by looking at them and using that sense. If you look into their eyes, you can often tell what they are, because their eyes can show their evil. If you have negativity toward someone however, your subconscious can make you see them as a negative figure anyway, or negative beings can use your dislike of the person to portray them as a sinister figure in order to fool you. So knowledge of the subconscious (egos) is vital.

Through the process of enlightenment, consciousness is gradually awakened. That means that you clear the consciousness of those elements (egos) that make up the subconscious. Then you are more aware in daily life and less interferes in your dreams.

The level of teachings that someone gets is entirely due to their capacity to understand and receive them, which is according to the level of spiritual development that one has. The way to get profound wisdom and understanding is to take up the spiritual path. The capacity for wisdom contained in the ordinary consciousness is very limited. The knowledge about oneself and life that is attainable is small compared with what is possible to achieve on that path.

On the path, spiritual beings influence the three-dimensional world through the higher dimensions, and hence influence the events of everyday life. They place events and situations so that a person can be tested, and they test how the person acts in relation to their inner states such as acting with anger or honesty, for instance. By doing this, spiritual beings can see how prepared someone is to receive true knowledge. It's not given just to anyone because then it is not valued and is easily trashed and abused.

Knowledge is given according to one's own merits, when some-one is prepared for it and has earned it. It's given according to the capacity and level of spiritual development of the person. Nasty, angry, and dishonest people for example are restricted in their capacity to receive true knowledge. If they reduce these defects properly, their capacity to receive knowledge can then be increased.

WHEN YOU CAN'T SEE CLEARLY
IN THE ASTRAL PLANE

Sometimes when getting into the astral plane you can't see at all or things look very dim. This is generally due to three things. The first is that the level of awareness in daily life and hence the level of awareness or consciousness while out of the body is low. If this is the case then it's a matter of correcting the problem: this requires practice to increase the level of awareness and exercises of self-knowledge and inner transformation.

The second reason can be that elements of the subconscious, ego states are interfering. This interference can be internal or external. If it's internal you need to deal with the ego state and if it's external use recitations and other protective methods I describe in chapter eleven of this book

Thirdly, it could be an outside sinister force or being that is interfering, in which case again, use methods of protection and ask your Being to help you—it helps to feel confident that you can overcome whatever you're facing.

CREATING YOUR OWN REALITY

Many who go into the astral plane are happy to be in the projections of their subconscious, often without knowing that what they are seeing is just a projection from within themselves; moreover, many like to imagine things and make them "real."

This can be done because thought is an energy which becomes like matter there for the traveler, but I wouldn't recommend doing this because it prevents you from seeing what's actually in the astral plane. The effect is something like a person who is taking drugs, who is hallucinating and missing reality. It's far more beneficial to see what's actually there.

One night while consciously in my astral body I saw a person I knew, I saw he was dreaming, and I asked him some questions. His responses were unclear, even nonsensical, and he eventually became confused. I then asked him about a specific object. I spoke to him about it later in the physical world, and while he vaguely remembered something in a dream, he was dreaming too heavily to be able to see and recall what was happening. At other times people have had better results, but it goes to show how strongly the subconscious states of the dreamer influences how much of the astral plane is actually seen.

To see what's there keep your level of awareness high, staying aware and staying out of any tendency to daydream. Being in mental images over there can mean losing awareness of the astral plane and falling into an ordinary dream. It's better to have real experiences; they mean so much more in the long run.

TIPS WHEN ASTRAL TRAVELING

∞ When you are flying to a place and encounter an obstacle, you should try to get out of it very gently. Avoid being confused by it; otherwise, you're likely to be back in your physical body immediately.

∞ Unless your intuition tells you otherwise, you shouldn't get distracted with what you see while traveling, because you can get sidetracked and you may not make it to your destination. Many astral traveling experiences come to an end in this way. You need to be disciplined and focused when you are traveling so that you get to your destination.

∞ If you're flying at a very high speed, don't be afraid about it—just go along with it. If you try to slow down or stop it, you'll probably be back in your physical body almost straight away.

∞ Thoughts about your physical body or worries of how you are going to get back can end your astral experience.

∞ If you arrive at a place and you can't see anything, try to be aware and look around, and if you still can't see anything, ask your inner Being to clear it, or use the recitations (which are explained in chapter 11).

∞ If you're in the astral plane and you can't see the place you want to get to, visualize the place again and you'll get closer to it or land there.

QUESTIONS AND ANSWERS

Why can't I see clearly?

It's due to the level of conscious awareness, but it can also be due to the interference from an inner state (ego) or an outside entity. If this happens again use a recitation of protection then you'll see more clearly, if this was the problem.

Why don't I have control of the movement of the astral body? In the first months it was very difficult to move the astral body; I was mostly floating above the physical body. It's only after one year that I started walking a little and flying, and spending more time in the astral plane.

It's because you need to increase your levels of concentration and conscious awareness. This will increase with the exercises and with the whole esoteric work. It also improves with experience.

It is very confusing that when I walk through the house in the astral plane I open the doors normally. How is it possible for the astral arms to touch and open the material doors? Doors which are closed physically seem to be open and vice versa.

You can open the doors because they are in the astral world and are made of astral matter, just as we can move things in the physical world with the physical body.

In the night I see very poorly, which is a problem. On the other hand, I wonder how I see and perceive the light since the astral eyes don't function with the light as the physical ones do. Is there any way to perceive the places and objects more clearly, with more light?

The astral eyes see astral things just as the physical ones see physical things, so you can see things just as clearly there as here. Clarity in the astral plane is usually due to the level of conscious awareness, or the interference of negative forces, psychological states, and what's being shown by higher beings. And also, the conscious awareness can be woken up by spiritual beings when they need to teach or show something.

The other night was the first time I have ever consciously got up in the astral plane. I made the conscious decision to gently roll out of bed. I wasn't even sure it worked, but then it was as if the lights came on and I was somewhere else. I took that little jump and floated along effortlessly through walls and any object. I went through a plate glass window and hovered above the trees. I did not know where to go since I did not know where I was. This confusion brought me back to the comfort of my bed. I went back in the astral several more times as I often do, but when I tried to pass through a different wall, I thudded to the floor. Is this common? What was holding me back the next few times? It was as if the walls were solid!

The problem with the wall was your mind; it was your doubts that caused that problem. Next time push into the wall with your hand so that it starts to go through, then follow through with the rest of your body.

Would you be able to come into contact with departed relatives or loved ones through astral travel?

You can come into contact with departed relatives or loved ones through astral travel, because a recently deceased person is in the other dimensions. But after they have died for some time you mostly see their personality, which is what would usually be the part most recognizable as the person. You can talk to them and they recognize you, but they are locked in the past and the consciousness is absent, as personalities are mental forms that can sometimes be sensed here, which is when they are referred to as ghosts. It is different in NDEs, where experiences are often given with deceased loved ones.

CHAPTER SEVEN

OVERCOMING SOME OF THE OBSTACLES TO ASTRAL PROJECTION

THERE ARE MANY DIFFICULTIES to face when learning to astral project and to sustain the ability. It's not easy to overcome them, but if you do you just might find success.

This may involve making sacrifices, and there's often a temptation to give up something when it seems like it's not working. But rather than giving up, it's better to see what the obstacles are, to persist, and overcome them. Then you'll get not only experience, but also the willpower that will help you in many avenues of life.

What sometimes seems like an insurmountable obstacle may be overcome with patience, effort, and spiritual change. You need to see the particular obstacles that you face in order to overcome them.

I'm going to mention some of the common problems that turn up; they can be overcome if you are willing to put some work into it, since it's likely to cost you effort, time, and determination. These are just a few examples—difficulties of all kinds arise in so many different ways repeatedly when you're trying to have astral experiences. Keep track of your main goal and work to overcome your obstacles, within whatever limitations you may have.

PRIDE

One of the biggest stoppages for profound spiritual experiences is pride; it can cause more harm than good for a proud person to have profound astral experiences. Pride bars the doorway to advanced spiritual development, as humility is a requirement for knowledge in the higher dimensions.

There are higher beings in the other dimensions and they have their requirements for those who receive their knowledge. It won't take too much before you encounter one or more of them while you are out of your body. The experiences of the higher dimensions then become not for pleasure or fun or having experiences, but discovering reality, notably your own, seeing the sad state humanity is in, realizing the wrongs you've done and maybe do, changing and helping others, and being a source of love and goodness into the world. If this sounds overly religious to some, then they should discover more, because it's like that in astral and near-death experiences.

The higher beings really don't give advanced knowledge to evil people, but give it according to grades of goodness.

So if you want to have higher spiritual knowledge, you'll need to recognize and get rid of pride in whatever form it emerges.

And know when you should keep silent about what you've seen over on the other side.

FEAR

Fear is a common problem when going into the astral plane or when trying to get there; it can be a big stoppage for many people. There are many different manifestations of it—fear of the unknown for example is very common—but you can learn to overcome the fear of being in the astral plane through experience, by studying your psychology to understand it and reduce the subconscious elements (egos), and also by strengthening your psychic energies through alchemy.

In the example of fear of the unknown, the more you do something or go somewhere and have no problems with it, the less fear is associated with that place or experience. You may be afraid of eating a piece of fruit that you don't know anything about for example. However, those who know about the fruit and know that it's fine can eat and enjoy it.

If you do the spiritual work you can understand, reduce, and eventually remove the different inner (ego) states. Fear is related to the overall state of the energies within the psyche. The exercise of alchemy transforms and strengthens the energies within the psyche. When the energies are weak there tends to be much more fear.

One of the biggest fears in relation to having OBEs is the fear that it is a dangerous thing to do and that it is dangerous to be there. However, it's worth bearing in mind that everyone astral travels every night when dreaming. When you astral project, you are aware of the whole process through which you (minus the physical body) go to the fifth dimension. When this process is new it can be very startling, and many people think that when they get into the astral plane they are not going to come back. But we come back every night after dreaming. It is a normal part of life to leave the physical body behind for it to rest and recuperate its energies—we couldn't survive if this didn't take place. It's just that with astral projection you are aware of the process that takes place when sleeping and leaving the physical body and going into the astral plane.

Another fear is that there can be sinister forces there that will stop you from coming back or will harm you in some way. There are beings of different kinds that exist in the astral world, but they will not harm you physically, so there is no need to worry about that.

LAZINESS

Laziness can be a very big obstacle; it's a problem not only for astral projection but also for spiritual development as a whole. At the same time you have to be aware not to force yourself with astral exercises.

Laziness in itself is an inner state, an ego that can trap anyone within the feelings that it brings. You can study and reduce it, but you should distinguish between laziness and actually not being up to doing an exercise, whether through illness, tiredness, other demands, emotional problems, stress, and any other issue. If in doubt, don't do it. You have to be sure laziness is the problem to do an exercise when you don't feel like doing it.

In the beginning, most who begin astral exercises are keen to try something new and eagerness continues if they see things are working. However, when experiences are not happening, they slow down, morale goes down, and reasons not to continue build up. Soon laziness and entropy settle in, practice gets forgotten, and eventually the person gives up.

If you've let the momentum slip and are out of practice, get back into it gradually and re-educate yourself. Start with an exercise for a very short period of time—up to ten minutes, but no more. If you do it any longer when you're starting back, the difficulties you may face can mean that you create an additional resistance to the exercises, so get back into it gradually but methodically.

By doing this you will bring back the mode and momentum of doing the exercises. Eventually you'll begin to see a light at the end of the tunnel and will gradually regain the momentum of practice.

FEELING DISHEARTENED

There's a big difference between reading, watching, and talking about astral projection, and actually doing it yourself. Sometimes expectations are different to reality and many discover that it takes a lot more work to astral project than they had thought. Experiencing astral travel can sound simple enough to do and yet it can be very difficult. It's easy to become disheartened, to think that you can't do it and to consider giving up.

But it's important to realize that it has to be learned, just like any new skill. You need to practice the exercises because it is a process of learning and training. You're unlikely to astral project as soon as you have the techniques, and even if you do, to repeat the success usually takes a lot of work, while maintaining the skill takes even more. But learn the exercises with patience, as learning any new skill takes time and practice. Consistent daily practice and a well worked out program makes all the difference.

It's important to get into a routine and build up, just like in sports. No one becomes good at sports overnight, and neither would someone who has been away from training be. They need to gradually get back into it, training themselves again until they reach the point where they left off, and improve from there. If you're consistent, you'll become good at it. You'll also learn how it works and gradually understand how you behave psychologically and physically when you're trying the exercises.

Problems at home, at work, illness, or even a visit somewhere for a period of time can sometimes throw your routine off, so you'll need to get back into the routine of practice whenever you're ready to.

Bear in mind there are higher beings influencing out-of-body experiences, and if you are not having them much, or if the experiences are not of a profound standard, it may be that you need to change what you do in your life and the way that you are.

PROBLEMS WITH PAIN, ILLNESS, AND TIREDNESS WHEN DOING ASTRAL EXERCISES

Feeling pain can be enough to stop any exercise of astral projection. Pain can commonly arise when you've been overdoing it, or when recovering from an illness, or simply when you're not used to the exercises.

If you've pushed yourself or forced your body to go through pain you can get to feel negative toward the exercises, so refrain from pushing yourself to the point of pain.

The body and mind should be trained to do the exercises gently and gradually, and the capacity of endurance varies from person to person. After an illness, the body is even more sensitive and vulnerable to pain and discomfort, and so greater care should be taken in those times. When you've been ill it won't take long to get tired or feel pain, so when you're ready to get back into practice, just try the exercises for very short periods of time, according to what your body can tolerate that is, before it becomes painful or uncomfortable.

After illness it would be best to start with very short relaxation exercises. Then if you are able, increase the time each day until you feel ready to practice fully, but never force your body. See what you can take and don't push it; build up gradually.

If you are simply trying to go back into the exercises because you have drifted away from them and you feel pain when you do them, the approach is similar. However, it will take less time to get back into the exercises since the body only has to be trained to remain still in a position for a while. At the same time, you'll need to go back to the discipline of focusing the mind on the exercises.

The main thing in both cases is to get started when you feel ready and gradually increase what you do according to your capacity.

Make sure you get enough sleep; you can't maintain a routine where you don't get enough sleep, and if you push yourself you can lose your capacity to function properly during waking hours—this can be dangerous and can even lead to illness. Factor in extra time to your normal sleeping time to do your astral exercises and always make sure you have enough sleep.

When it comes to astral exercises you have to watch that you don't force yourself, and increase the time spent practicing gradually, so that you get used to it. Stop if you feel you are forcing something or if the body feels uncomfortable with it.

ENTROPY

Entropy is a major factor in bringing down the momentum of astral exercises, but it applies to any activity. A new activity usually starts on a high note and progresses to a certain point. After that, things begin to slide downward until they reach the starting point. If the same or less effort is made through the life of an activity, it will inevitably slide back down due to the forces of nature. The way out of this is to apply an additional factor, usually an effort that brings the activity up in its notes, and like a musical scale, it can continue rising in higher octaves until another effort is needed, and so on. This counters the force of the entropy; if that extra effort is not made, things will go back to their starting point.

So when astral exercises are new it's interesting, you may feel eager to try them, make good attempts, and there may be some success. This eagerness continues if you see things working. But if things stay the same and extra efforts are not made, then inevitably experiences stop happening and the note goes down. It will fall back unless you review what you are doing and provide a higher octave with extra work. By doing that you can keep progressing, and this applies to any activity.

GETTING INTO A MODE OF PRACTICING

You should aim to get into the mode of practicing; when you get this right things just flow well, but it often takes considerable effort to achieve.

When you get fascinated with daily activities the mind is no longer directed toward spiritual development—it slips away, and its importance is easily forgotten or pushed to one side. But that doesn't mean that spiritual development itself has actually lost its importance, it's just that you're not aware of it. It's far more important than most people realize, and when this life is over it's what really matters. Time that is wasted is never recovered again.

DEDICATION AND DISCIPLINE

It's possible to have astral experiences here and there when trying to astral project, but for the astral exercises to work with any regularity, you have to be completely dedicated to them. To be able to project consistently requires very solid work throughout each day, and this means being disciplined and keeping yourself reminded of and focused upon spiritual development and astral projection in whatever you're doing.

Discipline in relation to the physical body is also very important for astral projection, since the body and the mind need to get used to a different way of approaching sleep. It takes a lot of work and willpower, but it does pay off.

If you can, always maintain your astral exercises. They will be the means with which you can investigate and experience spiritual realities and will allow you to acquire your own esoteric knowledge, far beyond what you can read in any book. You'll always remember your profound astral experiences and they will help you to get through the difficult times of life and the spiritual path, building the foundation of a faith that derives from knowledge and direct experience, which is something that very few people have.

THE ABILITY TO CONCENTRATE

A vital part of any astral projection program is the ability to concentrate upon the exercise you're doing, and so any program must include working toward developing this ability if it's to be consistently successful. If you don't, the mind will never be properly trained to be on the exercise you're doing, and then even the best techniques of projection are not very effective.

When you do your exercises and the mind keeps thinking about other things, it's usually due to a lack of practice in being focused during the day and it indicates you need extra practice in concentration or your practices need to become more consistent.

The concentration and visualization exercises can be incorporated into your daily program fairly easily, but it takes a great deal of willpower to be aware of yourself and what you're doing throughout the day.

BEING CONCENTRATED UPON
ACTIVITIES DURING THE DAY

If you can get used to being focused and concentrated upon what you're doing during daily life, then when you go to astral project, you're used to being on one thing and the mind is quieter.

When the mind is focused on one thing, it's not scattered in all kinds of different things. When it's scattered, you'll tend to think compulsively in a disordered way.

So if in your daily activities you do one thing at a time, and if possible finish it, or finish what you need to do on it before moving on to the next thing, you will create much more order and efficiency in your activities.

This also has an effect upon the quality and type of dreams at night. The important thing is to concentrate upon whatever activity you are doing at the time and to do only one activity at a time. Even if you have a lot of tasks to do and are under pressure, deal with the most important one, giving it your full attention, even if it is just for a few moments, before you have to do another task. Give your full attention to whatever you're doing at that moment.

Being concentrated on what you're doing goes hand-in-hand with observing your inner states. If you observe your inner ego states, such as feeling angry, tense, or afraid, and come out of them, you'll allow consciousness to get freer within yourself, and as awareness of the present moment is the default state of consciousness, you'll naturally be more aware of what you're doing.

Because of the demands of life it will be very difficult to achieve sustained concentration, so it may be a good idea to dedicate a certain amount of time to concentrating upon what you're doing; this could be one day on the weekend for example, or it could be for a longer time. Going on a retreat can be particularly useful for focusing the mind.

- projections of the subconscious
- Remember: Raom Gaom
- Fantasy (wanting) influences
dream ~ mind goes w/out
direction

CHAPTER EIGHT

DREAMS

EVERY NIGHT WITH SLEEP, dreams occur, whether they are remembered or not. In dreams what usually happens is that the process of thinking and daydreaming from the day continues, but without a physical body to bring us back to reality; therefore, the images from the subconscious become real for the dreamer, who exists in the model of the world that has been projected from the subconscious. Not all dreams are projections of the subconscious however, some are events actually taking place in the astral plane, some are a mix of actual events and subconscious projections, while others are scenes or places that are put there by one's own Being or by higher beings for the purpose of teaching.

LEAVING THE BODY AND
ENTERING THE DREAM WORLD

With sleep, we leave behind the physical body, which holds the psyche onto the three-dimensional world. We leave behind the sensory impressions of the three-dimensional world, and all there is of a person that is nonphysical enters the fifth dimension, usually the astral plane. The person is then connected to the physical body through a silver cord, which makes it impossible to not come back to the body after we have woken up.

So, while we dream, messages are sent from the person, the psyche, who is in the astral plane, to the physical body, including the brain and vice versa, through the silver cord. Although it is there, the silver cord is not normally seen when astral traveling.

Without a physical body, there is no physical world to see, touch, and taste, so what is left are thoughts, emotions, and consciousness, but you are in the astral plane. Unfortunately, when there (either when dreaming or when traveling consciously), what is actually in the astral plane is not normally seen, or it is only partially seen because of the images of the mind, which are projected onto it. Even if what is seen there is real, it's common not to even realize or question that you are there. It's the nature of that plane that we create our own world, which is not real. But there is something real there, only it is not normally seen when dreaming, or it's only partially seen through the haze of projected images. To see what's there, we must be clear of the images projected by the subconscious.

CLEARING THE SUBCONSCIOUS
DREAM IMAGES AND SEEING REALITY

When in dreams, the process of daydreaming that occurred during the day continues. Dreams occur at night because of the daydream of thoughts, images, and emotions of the subconscious (the egos) that take place during the day. Going through the day like that, one is rarely aware of the information of the five senses—of the reality of where you are at any given moment. Therefore, when sleep arrives, there is also a lack of awareness of where one is. What we do here we do there, and what we are here we are there. So if we bring awareness into our lives here, we bring it there as well.

Sometimes when dreaming you do actually see what is in the astral plane. It's because there can sometimes be periods of lucidity. In these periods someone may see what really exists in the astral world or dream about a place that actually exists in the three-dimensional world (even though they may never have seen it and discover it later in daily life). In these clear times it's possible to learn quite a lot; higher beings can show you things or teach you and they can awaken the consciousness, clearing the projections of the subconscious in order to teach something. As another example, you could also have a premonition about something that will happen in the future, something which you could have had no way of knowing, yet you may see the event in a dream and it comes true.

DIFFERENT KINDS OF DREAMS

Sometimes dreams themselves can have a symbolic meaning, so it's worth paying close attention to what you see either in dreams or when consciously in the astral world, because there may be important information, possibly in the form of a symbol, a number, an event, or words. Symbols are used because they are a universal language. Common symbols can be found throughout the great religions and mythologies of the world.

Information is often given there symbolically and the meaning of the scene or of the symbols shown in the dream can be intuitively comprehended, so it's very helpful to use intuition and to learn about the spiritual path and its symbolism, then you will be in a better position to decipher the correct meaning. You can learn to develop intuition just as you can learn to acquire other psychic abilities such as astral projection or remembering dreams.

Lucidity in a dream can be so great at times that you can actually realize that you're dreaming and realize that you're in the astral plane. You can be conscious in the astral in this way as effectively as if you had projected there. As discussed in previous chapters, this kind of experience is generally referred to as a lucid dream, but it's more accurate to say that you wake up out of a dream into the conscious experience of the astral plane.

Nightmares are another kind of dream; they are different from the usual bad dreams that many people have and I'll say a bit more about them later. Bad dreams, being chased, falling from heights, violence, and other unpleasant events are usually the result of what's happening within the psyche during daily life. Many negative states and strong emotions often go unnoticed during the day, but they manifest at night into these scenes.

DREAMS AS AN INSIGHT INTO YOURSELF

Dreams are an insight into our psychology: they are what we are, but stripped of the conventions and norms of psychology and the rules of the physical world, and having no physical body or forms to bring us back to reality. We can therefore learn a great deal about ourselves by studying dreams, from both the meaningful dreams and the ones created by the images and false scenarios projected by the subconscious. In this latter type, you may see yourself doing bizarre, or mundane things, or low things, perhaps being angry, fighting, or stealing. They could just as easily be ordinary things that you do daily, as things that you wouldn't

[handwritten margin note: Bad dreams reflect daily life]

84

usually do. In either case, bizarre though they sometimes may be, they are an accurate reflection of what goes on in the psyche, in the conscious and subconscious processes during any day of your life.

It's very useful to see these different psychological states (egos) during daily life and to study dreams to get information about the states such as fear, anger, or anxiety that occur during the day. You can also learn how to get rid of the different elements of the subconscious (egos) and to replace them with consciousness. As the subconscious gradually decreases, it helps you to be more conscious during both dreams and in daily life.

To choose which particular ego state to understand most urgently, look at your dreams to see what ego states are appearing in them—work upon them and clear from daily life anything that you see in a dream. So when you see an ego state during a dream, the next day, and from that day onward, study how that state works within you in daily life. If it looks like it's not appearing, increase your level of observation and keep watching, because it will appear—it may be in a subconscious way, but it will emerge at some time. The fact that you see it in your dreams means it's there in your subconscious. You'll have to be very strong willed not to allow ego states you see in dreams to continue manifesting in the physical world. If they do keep appearing, you should observe yourself more carefully to discover what you haven't previously known.

The less time spent in subconscious states and daydreaming in daily life, the more the psyche increases in its lucidity, and as a consequence, increases the lucidity of dreams, because they are directly related. In other words, the more aware we are in daily life, the more aware we are in dreams.

We come from the world that we dream in and return to it with death. However, we also return to that world every night, but because of incoherent dreams, it's not usually recognized. When

Psyche —▷ dream

daily life —▷ observe daily life

fix ~ observe daily life

someone has a clear out-of-body experience, they can see that world as it is. You might ask yourself what is real and what is temporary, here or there?

HOW TO REMEMBER DREAMS

There's much to be learnt from dreams; remembering them will give you an insight into your psychology and will get you used to the astral realm you're going to explore. Although much is projected by the mind, they can still occur in real places that you have traveled to in the astral plane from within a dream and you can get much information from their scenes, from the symbols in them, and from any teachings that may have been given.

It is easy to miss dreams, but by learning simple techniques you can remember them better. Try these techniques every morning when you wake up. The more you do them, the more you will develop your ability to recall dreams consistently; also, if you learn to increase your level of awareness during daily life, your dreams will become clearer.

∞ Plan ahead

Just before you go to sleep, have the intention to remember your dreams in the morning when you wake up, because as soon as you wake up, it's as though a little program starts in the head that reminds you to try to remember what you have been dreaming about. Normally the mind comes in and says "get up, shower, work" or whatever it is. If you've thought about that beforehand, it's become a routine. So what you need to do is to kind of re-educate yourself to think about remembering dreams when you wake up rather than other things.

∞ Lying still when you wake up

When you wake up don't move even a finger. Simply open your eyes and close them again and begin to remember your dreams from the first one you can remember. Try to see it in as much detail as you can, then you may find that more dreams appear. Carry on remembering the ones before if you can. It may take a bit of training not to move when you wake up, but if you try time and again, you'll begin to train your body.

It's important not to move when you wake up because by moving, the physical and astral bodies become merged, so you become locked into your physical body. Whereas when you just wake up, they often have a looser connection, which makes remembering dreams easier.

∞ Pronouncing the mantra Raom Gaom

If you still can't remember any dreams, continue to lie still for a little while with your eyes closed to see if any appear. If they don't, then pronounce this mantra. A mantra is a series of sounds, a word, or words that have psychic effects, just as music and other sounds do. Mantras have these effects depending upon the words or upon their sounds, which are often based upon the vowels A, E, I, O, and U. The sound of each of these vowels has a vibration, which affects the vibration of the psyche due to the law of vibratory affinity. Each vowel has a different tone and therefore has a different effect. Chanting mantras lightens your inner state and can increase your psychic faculties.

A good mantra for remembering dreams is called Raom Gaom. When you pronounce it, elongate the sound of each letter like this: *Rrraaaaaooooooommmmmm*

Gaaaaaoooooommmmm. You can listen to the sound file on the website to get a clearer idea of how it sounds.

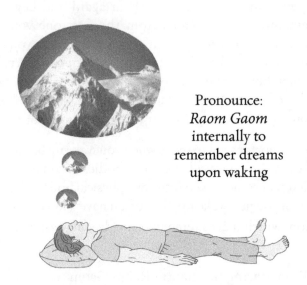

Pronounce:
Raom Gaom
internally to
remember dreams
upon waking

If you pronounce this mentally (not aloud) repeating it over and over again for a while, you'll notice the dreams beginning to appear. As they do, stop with the mantra and concentrate upon each one. Then if you need to, pronounce it again several times and try to remember more.

∞ Keeping a dream diary

You may find it useful to keep a diary or journal where you record your dreams, so when you've woken up and looked back over the night's dreams, you record them in your diary. It is so easy to forget a dream and you may find that things you don't understand now and would have soon forgotten may have significance for you later. You can also build an overall picture of your dream life, finding things that are repetitive, prominent, or important as patterns emerge over time, but make sure that no one else can see it or find it. This is because someone may find out things that are personal to you.

∞ Train dream recall by remembering events of the day

There's another exercise that's similar to dream recall, but it's like a dream recall of the day. At the end of the day, just briefly go back over the day, and that will help you to crystallize in your mind the things that have happened. This helps to train the memory in this type of recall and gets us to reflect upon the day.

When you look at what's happening in the day, look not just at the things you're doing, but also at the emotional states you had, and if you can, see if you can spot how they influence your dreams. It's these states which, if they're strong enough, produce much of the content of dreams.

∞ Be aware

The more we respond to environmental stimuli, the better we can remember dreams, and so the more aware we are in life, the more we are going to remember dreams. By practicing being aware and observing within, we come out of thoughts and daydreams and perceive the three-dimensional world. This clears the mind and that gives clearer dreams, which are easier to remember.

Having regular patterns of sleep and getting enough sleep also helps in remembering dreams. When you look into them, see what kinds of dreams you are having, and whether you can see any meanings or messages in them.

It's useful to look for anything in relation to self-knowledge or esoteric knowledge or anything that can teach you. Some useful things to watch out for include any ego states such as anger or fear, whether you've been to any real places, whether you have been flying or lucid, whether there are any symbols (symbols are a form of communication in the astral plane) that you can recognize and intuitively capture the meaning of, whether you had any teachings or even had mystical experiences, or whether the same dream recurs.

If you are in doubt about what you see and don't understand it, try using your intuition to work it out. Later, if you get more spiritual knowledge, you'll understand your dreams better.

QUESTIONS AND ANSWERS

Usually when I wake up I can't remember my dreams at all. Is there anything else I could try other than the mantra?

You need to practice the technique for remembering dreams; you'll train your memory with it and so it improves as you practice it. If you've just started practicing a mantra, you'll need to give it sufficient time to allow it to work, as it has a cumulative effect over days or weeks.

The reason why I can't remember some of my dreams is because they're always so abstract and unstable. The scenery is always warped and constantly changing and so are all the people as well as my emotions. Nothing ever stays the same for more than a couple of seconds and nothing seems logical or orderly.

You have to take what happens in dreams and the ability to remember them as part of an overall psychological and spiritual study. The reason why they are so abstract and unstable is likely to be because of the state of the psyche itself, as they reflect it.

With the right kind of spiritual practice you will be able to create more order within and have more coherent dreams. They are also related to the level of awareness you have in daily life: the more aware you are, the clearer that dreams tend to be.

I tend to remember my dreams and have been trying to write them down, which I am bad about not doing, but there was one I remember in particular in which I was flying around a very high mountain. I feel pretty sure it was in Tibet or that area. I remember becoming lucid and trying to change direction of my flight. I could not control it and then I lost the dream. Is this common? Is there something I could have done that might have helped me control this experience better or was I just not ready?

It's very common to lose an astral experience like that, particularly if you're not used to it. The more you do it, the more you'll learn how to stay there and to go where you want to. Treat it as a learning experience and see what happened at the point that you lost it.

Having more awareness while you are there and learning to concentrate when you want to go somewhere will also help, as will alchemy.

I'm aware that dreams of flying usually are astral travel, but my most recent one was of flying throughout a gigantic antique store, plus most of my dreams that really have left an impression on me have been dreams that deal with antiques. Do the antiques have any real significance?

Very much depends on the context of the dream. Intuition can usually give you the right direction—that's catching the first feeling you had about the dream when you woke up.

Antiques can be projections of your subconscious, or they can be more symbolic. For example, they could symbolize something ancient that you have to uncover about yourself, or could relate to the state of your spiritual development at present.

I awoke one morning early enough to practice the mantra. It seemed to work and I was remembering dreams—that is until I heard a voice so crystal clear that it seemed to be right beside my head in bed. It startled me so much that I jumped away from it almost in a fighting stance to protect myself. My question is, are voices such as this evidence of the astral?

They can be from the astral plane. Because you have been practicing for astral projection you are more receptive to the influences of the astral world, and you still had a slight connection to the astral world as your astral body had not quite merged with your physical one. Sometimes higher beings can speak and you can hear them like that. This is different to the voices of the ego states, which sound like yells, screams, etc., which are heard as they split from the physical body and go into the fifth dimension.

Maybe it's beginner's luck. Last night, I had two lucid dreams, including a flying dream. In the first, I was aware I was dreaming and able to direct it. I was able to focus sharply on things and even read small text, which didn't make much sense. In the second, I was able to fly where I wanted, for a while at least. My question is, what does this mean? It was a nice experience, and I will try to duplicate it, but what context is there for this and what is the next step? Also, doing the first exercise of remembering the dream before completely waking up has helped me to retain a good bit of it, though a lot has faded.

You are being helped to learn about the astral plane by spiritual beings or by your own Being. If you try the exercises determinedly and with a lot of patience, you can get a lot of help.

CHAPTER NINE

OUT-OF-BODY AND DREAM EXPERIENCES

MANY OF THE SYMBOLS in ancient sites and texts are depictions of actual symbols or experiences or processes found in the fifth dimension, usually the astral plane, but they are seldom understood that way because most trying to interpret them today don't have a knowledge of astral symbolism; at best they tend to read about other people's experience. To get personal knowledge of astral symbolism requires not only getting into the astral plane, but also getting access to its secret teachings—and that's not easy as the requirements are very difficult to meet.

Experiences in the astral world can be objective, or subjective, or a mixture of both. Moreover, the language of the astral world is often intuitive and symbolic, making it more prone to subjective interpretation.

You can get a better understanding of what happens in dreams and out-of-body experiences by increasing your experience and knowledge of the astral world. This will also help you to understand how to make best use of your time spent consciously there.

You'll also gain much more knowledge if you acquire self-knowledge, if you are aware of and clear many of the subjective elements of the subconscious, and embark upon the process of enlightenment.

To understand the meaning of dreams and out-of-body experiences, it helps to have conscious experiences of the dimension from which they arise, and have an understanding of the process of enlightenment. If you don't, you're more likely to give subjective interpretations to what you see, which anyone can give.

Additionally, it's important to be able to distinguish between the projections of the subconscious and a genuine symbol, for which self-knowledge is valuable. It is important to clear the psyche of its subconscious projections; the clearer and more objective the psyche becomes, the more objective are dreams and out-of-body experiences. Understanding them goes hand-in-hand with making the psyche more objective.

I give more information about the dimensions beyond this one and the astral plane's symbolism in my books and articles about the esoteric.

DREAMS AND EXPERIENCES FROM THE SUBCONSCIOUS

Much of what's seen in dreams and astral experiences in the beginning are the projections of the subconscious; use intuition to tell whether this is the case or not and where they are coming from. It's very important to learn about the subconscious and how the psyche works because then you can take the steps to clear the elements of the subconscious (egos). Without this, astral experiences are always subject to the subjective projections of the subconscious.

Also, there are often negative experiences in dreams and night-mares; these can be due to the state of the psyche and other more esoteric causes, all of which can be changed.

SYMBOLS IN THE ASTRAL PLANE AND IN DREAMS

Dreams and astral experiences often have a symbolic side. If you look at a dream plainly there may be nothing much to it, but when you recall your first intuitive feeling about it when you wake up, you know that it is referring to a certain aspect of your life—it's giving information about a person, a situation, etc., and you know what it is and what's going to happen. In this way, you gradually begin to interpret your dreams and astral experiences and the symbols in them. It's very useful for inner development, because as you gradually remember your dreams more and more, you'll intuitively know that a particular dream is telling you what aspect in your life you must change, what inner states you urgently need to work upon, which situations are harming you or are harming others, etc.

In the astral, a particular symbol may sometimes have different meanings and the right one can be grasped through intuition. It's important not to tell any personal esoteric teachings you may have had in the astral plane to anyone, because secrecy is very important there and if you tell others, you may not be shown any more for some time. This is known as hermetic silence.

USING INTUITION

It's useful to use intuition when interpreting the meaning of a dream or an astral experience because of the intuitive and sym-bolic nature of the language of the astral plane. Each symbol there can have many different meanings, and each is relevant to the individual who experiences them, even though there are symbols with universal meanings.

Intuition is a sense that allows us to capture information from a higher plane that could not otherwise be gained from the mind or from the five senses. The information reaches us from a spiritual part within that is located in the higher dimensions; it's one of several psychic faculties that can be developed.

Intuition works immediately. When you remember a dream you get a first feeling about what things mean. Go with that feeling without allowing the mind to come in and reason, because the ordinary mind lacks that higher connection.

We can be forewarned of danger and other things because events that are going to happen physically often take place in the higher dimensions first, and information from those dimensions can reach us here.

Everyone carries this sense to a certain extent and probably most have experienced it. The problem is that most people do not develop it or pay attention to it. But everyone has it, so try using it when you want to discover the meaning of a dream or an astral experience.

MEDITATING ON AN INNER STATE TO GET INFORMATION FROM DREAMS AND OBEs

I used to practice meditation on an ego state a lot; I would analyze a state such as anger or fear remembering as much about it as I could until I couldn't come up with any new information, my mind would get stuck like in a paralysis, become quiet, and that's where I would use the dream and astral world to get extra information about the inner state.

I would spend as long as I needed to in a meditation room analyzing and meditating upon ego states I had seen during the day. I used to sit up and meditate, then lie down to continue my meditation, and from there I would either drift in and out of sleep and dream or have an out-of-body experience—in either case I would often get information about the defect or ego that I had been trying to understand by meditating upon it. I could go up to eight hours at a time practicing like this, then take a break for ten minutes or so, and then go back into the room to do another practice for a few hours more. Not long after that I would start my practice of astral projection to go to sleep at night.

One time practicing meditation during the day with a group of people I had a strange experience. I was lying down and saw that one person was not in his sleeping bag or in the room, so I got up to take a look. Something felt strange, so I checked my body and it was solid, it was physical, nothing stretched, and I tried to jump to float but it didn't work. I thought I wasn't in the astral plane and I decided I would lie down to continue my meditation exercise and perhaps to have an out-of-body experience. As I lay down, I woke up without realizing that my body had been sleeping, and saw that the person was sleeping in the room—he hadn't gotten up after all. This illustrates how easy it is to be in the astral plane and believe it's the physical world.

Occasionally, when practicing astral projection, right at the moment that sleep arrived I would hear voices in my head that were like screams, moans, groans, etc. I could hear them as though they were real voices in the physical world, but although they were not physical voices, they were real nonetheless. They were ego states of fifth-dimensional matter that I had seen incorporating into me as a child each night as I fell asleep, which is a process that happens to everyone as their personality develops as a child. At the moment we fall asleep the various ego states detach themselves and it's possible to hear them in the state between wakefulness and sleep as they and we enter the fifth dimension.

LEARNING FROM DREAMS AND OBEs

Many astral experiences contain symbolism as it is the language of the astral plane. Symbols are sometimes a clearer and more direct means of communication than language.

I've used dreams and astral experiences to get knowledge for many years. Many of these experiences were in relation to my own ego states. I knew that whatever I saw about an inner state, even if it was in a dream, I had to try to understand about that state the next day, as I knew that whatever I saw in my dreams was the very thing that I needed to urgently correct.

Occasionally in dreams I would see people I knew from different times of my life. I saw how some friendships were created and sustained by inner ego states I had. But when I first saw this, I hadn't realized just how much of what was inside me psychologically affected what I did—I had thought that I did things according to the opportunities that were presented to me and out of my own wishes, but much had arisen from the ego states within me. I knew I had to get rid of them in order to stop repeating mistakes and to bring about new circumstances.

Dreams can teach much more than psychology, as they are a communication vehicle between this dimension and the next. Every time you dream you can potentially get information that will help you to understand something. This is why some ancient peoples valued them so much as a guide.

In dreams you can get premonitions, be warned of things you can avoid, get information about situations you're about to face, events that are going to happen in your life, about people you know, what people are thinking about you, what they're planning against you, and how to deal with situations. The possibilities are almost limitless, and the more you learn to use them, the more you begin to trust them because they are so accurate and precise, if you can interpret them that is.

The guidance and information you get applies to any avenue of life you can think of. For instance, you can be told about things that are happening far away and then you can wake up in the morning and discover they're true. Of course there's also a spiritual guidance you can get, which is of the knowledge of things that are beyond this world. You can be shown what people face after death, and you can get the same kind of knowledge that you can get while having a conscious out-of-body experience in the astral plane.

There are spiritual initiations, real ones that occur in the higher dimensions to test people for each stage on the journey to enlightenment; they are real, but you'll have to go through an initiation yourself to know they exist. They are a secret knowledge, hidden by the qualification of tests, and to acquire their qualities requires passing their tests. Every test takes place in a very clear dream state—it's like real life in that it's very clear, you are seemingly fully conscious, but you don't realize you're in a dream. The tests are on every aspect of yourself, your weaknesses to be overcome, actions to change, and so on. Everybody is being tested at some point in their life to see whether they are fit for the process of initiation and the solar journey to enlightenment and oneness, but everyone is unaware of it. Dreams help you to see what processes you are going through spiritually in this life and as a preparation for existence beyond that.

I can't begin to explain all the things that can be learnt with dreams, there's just so much, but if you remember them in the morning, study them in great detail, and write them down if you think you need to. They might be vague in the beginning and you might not understand what's going on in them, but as you persist and you understand how to interpret their symbolism, you find you have a daily guide to your life that you learn to value and trust, and when you go into the astral plane, you get to be there at the source of that guide, in the dimension where that learning originates.

A MEDITATION TECHNIQUE I WAS TAUGHT IN THE ASTRAL PLANE

There are many kinds of spiritual experiences you can get when traveling out of the body. About two years after I began practicing astral projection I had an experience in Egypt.

One night in the astral plane I found myself walking in a corridor made of stone. There were life-sized statues of what appeared to be Egyptian deities, and the light was subdued but clear. Directly in front of me was a door; a figure wearing a ceremonial headdress opened it for me and I walked in.

Inside I was astonished to be in a temple room like a spiritual practice room. The walls were again made of stone but the light was brighter, and there were statues and symbols around. Sitting up against a wall were spiritual beings wearing Egyptian ceremonial outfits. Each sat with their legs together and knees up, unlike the Oriental cross-legged position. I recognized some but not all of them from pictures of statues and hieroglyphs of ancient Egypt. They sat motionless and in silence. It was a beautiful and serene environment.

Another figure, a spiritual being, came up to me and took me to a granite pedestal, which had a bowl carved out of the top of it. There was water in the bowl. He gestured toward an opening in the wall near the bowl—it was a small, long passageway that had been carved through the stone, which went upward at an angle for a long way, and as I looked up into it I could see stars in the night sky.

I looked into the water and contemplated; in the water was the reflection of the stars and I felt an invitation to meditate upon them. I stilled my body and looked at them intensively and they began to take on a magical quality as though they were animated, and the water seemed to swirl as though in a spiral of creation. At that moment I lost consciousness of my surroundings and felt myself flying backward at high speed as though in a vortex and suddenly came back to my body and merged into it.

Many years later I read there are actually shafts in the pyramids and they point to significant stars, which I hadn't known at the time. With some innovation, it would be possible to build something simple that would make it possible to do this meditation exercise. There is also a description of an exercise of astral projection by the Essenes describing how they used to concentrate on the stars and project into the celestial realms.

EXTRATERRESTRIAL CONTACT IN OUT-OF-BODY EXPERIENCES

It's possible to have contact with intelligent extraterrestrial beings by having out-of-body experiences. Just as we have access to higher dimensions, so too do they. While many astral experiences with extraterrestrials are no doubt imaginary and figments of the subconscious, there are also some that are real.

Real ones can contain experiences that can only happen with extraterrestrial contact, such as being taken to real places, and seeing verifiably real things the astral traveler would otherwise have no knowledge of and by communicating with extraterrestrial beings who can give unexpected knowledge, which would have been impossible to have known otherwise.

I've known numerous examples of this. I've also spoken to someone who has seen a symbolic language in an astral experience with extraterrestrials, which they later traced in accounts of people who had physical encounters with extraterrestrial craft, and who described and drew an identical language.

Advanced beings know of the existence of higher dimensions and they use them; it's we as a humanity in our ignorance that have closed ourselves off from our innate but latent faculties that enable us to experience higher dimensions.

I've had lots of astral contact with extraterrestrials, and they have only been benevolent beings with great knowledge, who respect the free will of others, and who live in harmony with the universal laws of creation and enlightenment.

There are many things someone could do to have extraterrestrial contact, but the most effective is to personally be going through the process of enlightenment. The reason for this is that many extraterrestrials are going through this process of enlightenment too, and thus share a common life goal and set of principles with those that are also going through this process. There is a shared knowledge, and to a degree, a sense of trust they don't have with the average person who doesn't share the same principles and who may potentially act in a negative way. They occasionally seek out those taking the spiritual journey and contact them—I've spoken to someone who has been pulled out of their physical body by different extraterrestrials a number of times while falling asleep and taken places where they were shown amazing things. Spiritual in this sense is not a set of beliefs but a way of being and living.

Anyone who can tune in to them in thought and consciousness can potentially contact them though, as time and distance are not as they are here in higher dimensions. But the thought and consciousness must be of similar spiritual affinity to theirs to be able to connect with them.

Another way they may be interested in astral contact, or even physical contact, is if a group of people gather for spiritual purposes and make attempts to contact them. This works because thought is fifth-dimensional, and it travels in waves—they may pick up on it when they are conscious in the astral plane or through telepathy. Telepathy involves being aware of receiving fifth-dimensional signals while conscious in the three-dimensional world, which works because our psyche consists of different parts which exist in different dimensions.

QUESTIONS AND ANSWERS

In a recent astral experience, I was taken somewhere and I was shown some things I didn't understand at the time. The first was of what appeared to be an ancient wall. On this wall were round objects that upon closer observation became scenes of different people and different times. The only thing that comes to mind is the Wheel of Samsara. Was this an esoteric symbol to teach me?

Yes, this very much sounds like symbols that were used in the astral world to teach you. If you don't understand them now, remember them well, so that later if you continue this work and your knowledge increases, you will find that you can understand the things which seemed to be obscure in the beginning.

Does the infinity symbol have any significance? Likewise, does classical music have any significance?

The infinity symbol is a true esoteric symbol; it means endlessness, cycles that come back upon themselves. It also represents the cycles of evolution and devolution, which travel round and round from existence to existence. The spiritual awakening is needed to get off this cycle.

The symbol can be found in the Ninth Sphere; in the right context if you see that symbol it could mean that the work with alchemy needs to be carried out.

Classical music can often be spiritual. There is music in the higher dimensions, which can be significant when you hear it.

When you say not to mention anything about these symbols, does that include to you in these questions and answers or just in my everyday life? I've had no real new experience since this one. Is this because I spoke about it (also I've been quite sick and run down with a bad toothache so hopefully this is the reason)? Because of the above, I didn't do my exercises for about a week; I see what you mean about losing what you built up very quickly.

It includes everyone, but you should distinguish between ordinary experiences and the proper esoteric ones.

Both illness and speaking about personal esoteric information can bring about a loss of valuable experiences.

When the continuity in the exercises is lost, it needs to be built up again. Don't force the body to practice when you are ill though—wait until you are well enough to practice astral projection.

A comment of yours in your lecture on dreams struck me as being strange at the time. You said that it may be useful to keep a diary of your dreams but to keep it secret. If I see symbols in the future and keep a record of them, is this okay as long as I keep it secret?

Yes, you shouldn't have any problems with writing things in a diary as long as you keep them secret. Putting them in a code known only to yourself can help too.

I've heard that you should be careful when shape-shifting in the astral because you could come back with a part of that animal and start developing some of its wild characteristics. I would really appreciate your comments on this. Is there danger there?

No, you can't come back as an animal by doing that; what you are doing has nothing to do with the process of birth and death. You would do best to forget about shape-shifting because it is a projection of the mind. You would do better if you were to go into the astral plane being clear of those ideas and get real spiritual teachings.

Are there any moral implications to mystically uniting with a soul on the astral plane who is married here in this world?

Yes, I wouldn't advise that be done—there are spiritual implications to it. If you read my esoteric work, you'll see why I'm saying that.

Are there any rules that we should follow when in the astral world. I don't want to get there and do something that will offend anyone or anything!

Although you can use your common sense and intuition, you do need to know much more about what's happening in the different dimensions to know what's best to do and what not to do.

Can I move forward or back through time to any period I wish? If this is so, can I go back in time and change events, like preventing myself from making a bad decision?

You can go back in time in a way, because everything is recorded in the akashic files of nature, but you step into records of what has happened, not into real life, so you cannot go back in time to change past events.

The future is not recorded in the same way as the files of nature as it hasn't happened here. And, although events may permeate down the different dimensions, until they reach here, much is changeable.

Although you can see events that have yet to happen while in the astral plane (because events other than some accidents can be known in the higher dimensions first), it's often not 100 percent certain that all of the events of the future that are seen there will happen, because it is possible to change circumstances here in daily life and that alters what will eventually materialize. What usually happens though is that things don't change here, and what is seen there materializes here. This is when premonitions happen in dreams and OBEs.

Can drugs (alcohol, marijuana, psychedelics) help you get out of your body?

They can damage your astral and physical bodies, make the mind and emotions more active, and can make your consciousness more asleep, all of which are not good for continuing astral success, not to mention spiritual development. Some cultures use them to have experiences, but drugs drag you down to the inferior astral where you might get experiences that look spiritual, but which in fact belong to the negative side. Drug-induced experiences tend to intensify the negative side, so I wouldn't recommend them.

How do I ask for help from my guides when I am trying to project?

Presuming that you mean beings that have awakened for light, you can try to call on a spiritual being or angel by calling out their name. You could also ask for help and guidance from your own Being.

CHAPTER TEN

THE INFLUENCE OF
THE PSYCHE

The state of the psyche profoundly affects dreams and out-of-body experiences. It can be thought of as comprising the whole of what a person is psychologically: the mind, consciousness, emotions, feelings, subconscious, and personality.

It's a compendium of elements that have their roots in different dimensions. A knowledge of it can enable a greater understanding of what to do and what to take into account when exploring the fifth dimension.

THE STATE OF THE PSYCHE

The state of the psyche is the determining factor in what is experienced in astral travel, dreams, and out-of-body experiences.

That's why it is so important to understand the different cognitive factors that affect astral and dream experiences.

To have value, astral and dream experiences need to be both objective and meaningful. By objective I mean that what is experienced is true, real, and not simply a projection of the subconscious. By meaningful I mean that the experience is of value in a spiritual sense. I use the word spiritual in a wide sense here to include the search to discover important information about oneself, about life, and the way things work that are extra-sensory in their nature.

To look at the different parts of the psyche in order to understand more of what I'm describing, you could have a look at my book on self-knowledge—one of the most important aspects in it is self-observation, the ability to observe how we think, feel, and act.

If you observe inside yourself, you will explore your psyche and see how it works and you will realize how it relates to the astral plane and dreams.

THE COMPONENTS OF THE PSYCHE

The brain is the vehicle that allows the psyche to exist and function in the physical world, but the psyche is not simply the result of the processes of the brain, it exists in the absence of brain activity as can be seen in near-death experiences. At the same time, the psyche cannot exist in the world without a brain, and neither can consciousness develop without it.

The mind or the psyche is the intermediary between that which sees and what is seen. Between form and consciousness is the mind; likewise, between the five senses and consciousness is the mind. It is the instrument which enables consciousness to interact in form and enables consciousness to become aware of its own existence in the dimensions.

For the purpose of understanding astral projection, the psyche can be divided into different components:

∞ THE CONSCIOUS MIND – the conscious cognitive faculties, the intellect, the seat of thought, and the ability to reason, remember, plan, concentrate, visualize, and daydream. There are both higher and lower mental types, corresponding to higher and lower mental bodies in the mental plane of the fifth dimension. The nature of the human mind is what separates a human from an advanced animal.

∞ EMOTIONS – feelings linked to the stimulation of the nervous system and hormones. These are part of the survival mechanism in animals. There are higher and lower emotions, corresponding to higher and lower emotional bodies in the higher and lower astral planes of the fifth dimension.

∞ SEX – sexual feelings that drive the creative process.

∞ INSTINCTS – inherent repeated behavior that is fixed, not based on learning, and is inherent to the organism.

∞ ACQUIRED MOVEMENTS – learnt movements such as driving a car or playing a musical instrument, skills like typing, etc.

All the above are necessary for the human being to exist and live in the physical world.

> THE SUBCONSCIOUS OR EGOS – separate mental forms created from sexual and mental matter, which are built upon the above parts of the psyche. They work beneath the conscious awareness and become part of thoughts, emotions, movements, instincts, and sexual feelings. Examples include irrational

worries, callous greed, and sexual perversions. They are not necessary for human existence and are detrimental to it. They can be removed from the psyche.

THE PERSONALITY – the cognitive processes we acquire within one life, and the means of expression for the individual; the sum of the human parts.

THE CONSCIOUSNESS – the essential part of what a person is. It is that which experiences, it is what is "awake," and it contains all the spiritual qualities including peace.

Thoughts, feelings, and emotions are temporary, they pass; it is consciousness that is permanent, and it survives after death when all else is gone.

For spiritual development to have any lasting worth, it must develop and transform consciousness. Consciousness permeates thought, emotion, and feeling, and influences them. It gives spiritual feelings, which give direction to thought to initiate the processes of spiritual change, such as doing spiritual exercises.

If you can, find the peacefulness of the spiritual consciousness within yourself—it will lead you along the path to higher spiritual consciousness—it is your guide.

I'll expand upon the last three components, the egos, personality, and consciousness, as they are important to understand for spiritual development and are often overlooked.

THE SUBCONSCIOUS, THE EGOS

Thoughts, emotions, and feelings are transient and keep changing. The psychic centers of thought, emotion, instinct, sex, and movement are not stable or constant in their functioning and a multitude of different desires, drives, and feelings come and go.

This multitude is actually separated into individual forms in the fifth dimension, which can be referred to as "egos," as they all have a sense of "egocentric me" to them.

In each of these egocentric me elements is trapped a small amount of consciousness, which gives them their own life. They enter the psyche one at a time and exist in the fifth dimension, feeding from the energies of the psyche like parasites.

It's sometimes said that a person has a strong ego, but in reality each person contains a multitude of different states, which all have the continuity of the feeling of "I" or "me" in common. At one time someone may be full of pride, or anger, or jealousy, or fear for example, but soon afterward that state can be gone only to be replaced with another. One enters, then another, and so on endlessly. An inner state is rarely the same for long, unless they are particularly powerful, then ones such as fear or depression may last for a long time.

There are many ego states that everyone would feel better off without. There are ones that make life miserable such as worries, stress, depression, fear, etc., and there are states that cause harmful actions such as stealing, violence, fraud, gambling, arguments, and so on. The multiple ego states constitute the subconscious; they appear not to exist until circumstances or memories allow them to enter.

All of them can be observed, understood, and eventually removed. You may think that they are permanent parts of you and are necessary for your functioning; however, it's not true. Each human being has the capacity to observe and then remove them and to replace them with a different way of being, with the qualities of consciousness and higher mental and emotional centers such as intelligence, wisdom, and love. With the egos there is no peace; they have to be absent for true peace to occur.

The egos are based upon the psychological things needed by animals for their survival, which is why some human behavior can look animalistic. They are modifications of the original energies of the psychic centers, of thought, emotion, sex, movement, and instinct.

These states manipulate a person; they are a pawn of nature's program which keeps animals locked into a program of behavior, so that they can survive and be part of the whole natural process, without any need or wish for self-conscious activity. That program of nature forms the basis of human behavior.

That's why amongst people there's so much greed, anger, argument, and war. Each person is struggling to find their way in life, with no real purpose to it and all are driven by nature's program.

There's so much within that's unknown or shut off from conscious awareness. If you observe inside and see the different ego states, you'll see more and more of what exists within your subconscious, in its various levels of complexity. In this way you gradually begin to be conscious of the elements that make up your subconscious, and with further techniques, you may be able to increase your level of consciousness.

Often these different ego states are shut off from being the causes of actions in everyday life, as society restrains their expression, but they arise in dreams, where the norms of society are taken away and the subconscious roams, living out its fantasies, pleasures, and fears.

By looking into dreams, the reality of the psyche is laid open. It would be to turn away from reality to avoid acknowledging the experiences of dreams. It's far better to see what is within, to understand it, and if possible, be free of it.

In dreams the subconscious ego states are free to roam and project their scenes onto the astral world, which then form dreams. Ego states can be removed though, and the more that are, the freer a person is from their influence, and then dreams and astral experiences become clearer and more objective. This reduction of the subconscious also affects waking life in the three-dimensional world. The less a person is submerged in their egos, the less low vibratory states they exist in, and so the greater clarity of higher feeling, peace, and perception they feel.

The clarity of consciousness during daily life is directly related to the kinds of dreams a person has. The freer a person is of subconscious ego states during the day, the less those states produce bizarre, dark, bad dreams, and the more spiritual and clear the dreams and astral experiences become.

Feel the spiritual sense of stillness within yourself, the inner you, the consciousness. Let it guide you through your day, and observe every ego state that tries to take you away from it. This is how you will get knowledge from life and how you can advance with spiritual awakening.

THE PERSONALITY

The personality constitutes what's acquired in the normal course of development in one life. It is formed by the age of seven and by then we are recognizably the person we are today, and even though we may have changed in many ways, we are recognizably the same person as then.

The personality is a vehicle for the psyche to express through; it is formed by the experiences of life and includes all the skills that are acquired, such as walking, reading, talking, etc. Without this, the psyche would not be able to function in the world. The egos and consciousness exist from life to life, whereas the personality is formed in one life and is discarded thereafter.

Each personality develops uniquely according to the circumstances of a person's upbringing, and the place and era of birth, the parents, family, the egos, etc., affect its development.

Different personalities have different egos that predominate. When it is said that someone has a proud personality for example, it is not the personality that is proud, but that the personality is a vehicle or the means through which the ego of pride expresses itself, perhaps through mannerisms or words or gestures.

Each of us has a different personality because it is shaped by our early experiences in life, such as what our parents taught us, the school we went to, the friends we had, the books we read, etc., but it is useful to us only for one lifetime and is acquired only in one lifetime. Once this present life is over, it is discarded at death and that personality gradually disappears as the physical body disintegrates in the grave.

These personalities of the deceased are what people commonly refer to as ghosts. They are personalities left behind by people who passed away. That is why they are normally found in places where the deceased used to live. They exist in the fifth dimension and are formed from mental matter; they gradually dissolve with time after death.

The personality is needed to be able to function in this world and to interact in life, and it is the means of expression of the psyche, but it is the consciousness and the egos that are the most important for understanding the nature of the psyche in the astral plane.

CONSCIOUSNESS

Consciousness is the spiritual part, the immortal essence of a person. All spiritual growth, true wisdom, intelligence, love, peace, and mystical experiences emanate from consciousness. It gives the awareness of life.

During the day, self-awareness and the resulting peaceful stillness within is related to the clarity and nature of experiences in dreams or in the astral plane.

Consciousness is of the sixth dimension, a spiritual realm. It merges with the emotional and mental bodies in the fifth dimension and all three merge with the physical body in this one.

Being in inner peace with the ability to understand and feel higher emotions would be the best way to live, but the egos with their lower drives interfere and they scatter thoughts, permeating them with negativity, and submerge the peacefulness of consciousness in abysmal states.

Acting and responding to the world with the influence of consciousness is the highest way of being. When we respond to a situation with this, the response is intuitive and intelligent. It gives the ability to look objectively, freed from lower drives and influences. This allows intelligence to function and you can comprehend issues without the complications of the egos affecting thoughts and emotions.

With consciousness sufficiently developed, the psyche becomes permeated with spiritual feelings and then thoughts become directed toward spiritual awakening. Consciousness contains all the psychic faculties such as intuition, and all spiritual senses—it just requires bodies in the different dimensions for it to manifest.

Being conscious of the psychic centers of thought, emotion, sex, movement, and instinct uncovers the ego states in the subconscious; this is called self-observation. Being in self-observation is important for any given situation; then we are able to respond to it correctly, without the bias of ego-driven emotions, or rigid points of view, etc. When we are freed from the subjective viewpoints of the egos, we are free to see reality as it is—the greater the percentage of consciousness that's free of ego states, the greater the ability to perceive reality.

Perception is the natural state of consciousness, but it's passive. Activating it requires volition, which is self-remembrance, but you have to be able to observe yourself naturally or you will soon forget to do it.

The heavier the inner state, the greater the likelihood of forgetfulness is, and this forgetfulness weighs heavily upon the whole of the human race.

The sleep of perception is being in the state of forgetfulness, and that is to be submerged within the heavy states of the subconscious. The weight of the egos, the subconscious, is a burden to bear—it drags the consciousness down and the mind turns around and around and you can neither see, nor consider to look. And the burden drags us down into the cares and worries of everyday life and it stops us from seeing, it stops our perception; our perception is vital for our whole life.

It is not surprising that so few people take up this spiritual path, because the heaviness of what is inside of everyone is too great. But an inner awakening is necessary and that is to wake up, to perceive, and to see.

When you see within, which is to observe the ego states and be aware of them as they arise, and if you don't sustain them, but remove them, then you'll naturally have moments of peaceful awareness.

 Learn the difference between thinking about observing and actually doing it, because if you think about it you will have to keep directing your awareness with thought, and that is unsustainable. If you try to think yourself to be aware of the outside world, you will lose awareness of your inner states, and will have to keep trying to sustain thoughts of being aware, which in the long-run is impossible. Moreover, you will enforce a sense of "me" being aware, which is to feed an underlying pride. So learn how to perceive naturally; then both the inner and the outer become one.

Enjoy walking in peaceful inner quiet when the opportunities arise, but observe yourself through life and allow the peace within to manifest; then let that peace guide you in your spiritual life.

By being self-aware and clear of ego states we naturally live in the present moment and consciousness wakes up. When we are lost in a thought or a daydream, the mind takes us where it will on its scattered path, often at the drive of an ego state. Ego states keep the inner vibrations low, which brings compulsive thoughts, increases the daydreaming, and removes our psychological presence from the physical world, submerging us into strong imagery and an inner world dominated by the drives of subconscious ego states. In this state the consciousness, the spiritual within, is dormant. Most of the time is normally spent in the daydream of the mind and in subconscious states.

The consciousness trapped in an ego can be freed with the elimination of the particular ego that traps it. It then goes back to merge with the rest of the consciousness and consciousness increases. As it does, so does the capacity to be quietly at peace in daily life. There is a gradual waking up of consciousness, both in daily life and in dreams, because the level of consciousness here in the three-dimensional world is directly related to the level of consciousness in dreams. Consciousness is trapped in the subconscious and is small in proportion to the subconscious, and so most activity takes place in a daydream fueled by ego states.

Therefore, for more spiritual astral and dream experiences, inner states should be observed and ego states removed. The less ego states, the clearer the consciousness is of all the incoherent subjective illusion and the clearer the experiences are. The more egos are present, the stronger and more compulsive are the projections of the subconscious.

Consciousness is a tiny part of a greater Being which exists in higher dimensions, but which is not present within a person who hasn't created the conditions within for it to manifest. It emerges from the source, the Absolute, as one and divides as it enters creation. The Being has many parts; to truly awaken spiritually, each of these parts needs to merge one by one with that basic consciousness until they all re-merge back into one and return to the source with the knowledge of existence from being in creation. This is a long and difficult process.

As the consciousness is merged with superior spiritual parts then true peace is found. A person with basic consciousness can only feel a comparatively incipient, but important peace emanating from it. Truly profound peace in daily life is possible when the spiritual parts of the Being are merged with basic consciousness—when a person transforms the nature of their consciousness, merges it with superior spiritual parts, and advances toward peace and oneness.

THE DIFFERENT PARTS OF THE PSYCHE IN DIFFERENT PLANES

The different parts of the psyche reside in different planes and the essential processes of the human mind give continuity of self through the different dimensions. In the three-dimensional world while we are awake, we have the physical and vital bodies, consciousness, thoughts, feelings, instincts, and emotions, and a personality which we express ourselves through.

When we go into dreams or consciously into the astral plane, we leave behind the physical body in the third dimension and the vital body in the fourth dimension. We are then there as the psyche minus the body.

In the three-dimensional world we can only see physical manifestations of the psyche; you can't see someone else's thoughts for example. That's because thoughts take place in higher dimensions, and because the dimensions interpenetrate each other, thoughts have an effect on the physical body. The physical body is basically a vehicle for the other parts of the psyche to manifest in the three-dimensional world. Bodies are vehicles for the psyche and the spiritual within to exist in the dimensions.

Each dimension and plane from the third to the seventh has less laws than the preceding one. That's why we can fly in the astral plane for example—there are fewer laws constraining us.

From the sixth dimension onward are the truly spiritual dimensions and planes. There are also inferior dimensions, or hells, that have more laws than the third dimension.

In the dimensions, a person normally has the following:

THIRD DIMENSION:	The physical body
FOURTH DIMENSION:	The vital or etheric body
FIFTH DIMENSION, ASTRAL PLANE:	The astral body (emotions)
FIFTH DIMENSION, MENTAL PLANE:	The mental body (thoughts)
SIXTH DIMENSION, CAUSAL PLANE:	Consciousness

Additionally, a person is linked through the inferior dimensions to the center of the earth, the source of nightmares and hell.

Note that the astral and mental bodies are normally not true bodies. They are lunar phantom bodies that are basically just a shell or covering of the egos.

So when we sleep or astral project or have any other out-of-body experience, we are leaving the physical body behind in the three-dimensional world (and leaving the vital/etheric body in the fourth dimension) while the parts of the psyche that belong to the dimension we go into and above, stay with us.

THE EGO STATES IN THE FIFTH DIMENSION

When we go into the astral plane we have the consciousness, personality, and egos, within the astral and mental bodies. The egos belong to two planes of the fifth dimension: the astral and mental planes. The mental plane is higher than the astral one and has more freedom, but neither planes are exclusively spiritual as they contain egos and negative forces.

The egos work from the astral and mental planes of the fifth dimension and manipulate the physical body. They then give rise to different sensations in the psyche and in the body; they can make the heart beat faster, release adrenaline, produce trembling sensations, give rise to certain brain activity, etc.

Each of the different egos residing in the fifth dimension is a completely separate entity. They enter and leave a person, working through the fifth dimension to the third dimension according to the opportunity being available to them, and they take their food from the person's psychic energy. They enter the person one at a time in precise places in the psyche where, if you are observant, you can see them. When they leave, another ego comes in, which can even override or contradict previous ones.

Sometimes when falling asleep, particularly if trying to astral project, you can hear the noise when the egos leave the physical body for the fifth dimension. This can consist of moans, screams, shouts, babble, and so on, which is heard as though they were physical sounds.

Children whose personalities are not yet fully formed can sometimes see the different egos that have not yet been able to get into them, usually before sleep at night. These appear as ghostly shapes and forms, sometimes amoeba like, each with its own life. They wait for the personality to be sufficiently mature before they can enter.

It is possible to investigate and see the different egos separately in the mental plane. Through this you can discover much about how they work.

In the astral plane they can appear as entities separate to the person, in which case one may see something that looks like them doing an action of the ego, or incorporating into them, or the egos may appear symbolically as animals. Usually though, the person just has them inside as they do in the physical world, but mostly with less control as there is no physical world to ground a person in forms of substance.

The egos also work to influence what is seen in the astral world and dreams, and create whole scenes and events that are no more than projections of the egos—a false world. If someone is awake and conscious in the astral plane, freed from the projections of the egos and seeing the astral as it actually is, they can see a dreamer looking like a drunken person who can't seem to see properly; it's as though they've taken hallucinogenic drugs. Someone who is conscious in the astral plane at that moment might be able to get something through to them which they will remember when they wake up in the morning, but even then it's usually recalled within their own self-created dream world. Only in times of clarity can objective astral experiences be had. A person can even be projecting spiritual-like things that are no more than creations of their subconscious. That's why it's so important to study and understand the subconscious.

Without understanding the subconscious, a person has to rely upon the occasional times when they have moments of clarity in their astral experiences. Even so, negative forces can also use a person's egos to deceive the inexperienced astral traveler.

Dream or astral experiences can sometimes be made clear by the intervention of spiritual beings or by one's own Being when a person needs to be taught, even though their psyche may normally be very much dominated by their subconscious.

Anyone who is interested in understanding their psyche can learn a lot from remembering dreams and studying the different egos that they see in them, as there they act freely without the restraints of the physical world.

THE PERSONALITY IN THE FIFTH DIMENSION

This is basically the vehicle through which consciousness and the egos manifest, so it goes into the fifth dimension with the rest of the psyche. It is left behind with death, or when someone goes to a dimension above the fifth.

CONSCIOUSNESS IN THE SIXTH DIMENSION

Ordinary human consciousness is present in the sixth dimension, which is a spiritual dimension. The consciousness is normally the only spiritual part that a person has, but there are other parts that are separate from it that never manifest within a person unless they have created a suitable body (vehicle) which they can manifest into. These are the parts of the Being that divided at creation.

For a spiritual part to manifest within a body, a person has to have a high degree of spiritual purity, which is tested in the higher dimensions through the process of initiations in the process of enlightenment.

The spiritual part of the Being that incarnates in the sixth dimension is the Soul, known as the Son and also as the Christ in its higher aspect.

THE BEING IN THE SEVENTH DIMENS

The seventh dimension is the region of the spirit wh
and female aspects of the Being reside. In their initi
are the male Spirit and female Spirit, and in their highest stage
they are known as the Father and Mother. They are not present in
a person who has not integrated them within their consciousness
in the process of enlightenment.

References to these different dimensions and parts of the Being
exist in ancient texts, and I explain more about them and how they
relate to the process of enlightenment in other books.

BODIES IN THE HIGHER DIMENSIONS

A body is a vehicle that allows the psyche to manifest. The consciousness (the essential and most fundamental part of every
person) needs to be in the three-dimensional world so that it can
awaken. Through the evolution of life, the thoughts, emotions, and
personality allow the consciousness to function and interact in the
three-dimensional world until it is mature enough to liberate itself
from nature (to achieve enlightenment).

The bodies that a person is born with are a physical body, a
vital body, an astral body, and a mental body. Unfortunately, these
bodies are very limited in what they can do; the astral and mental
bodies are little more than a covering of the different subjective,
subconscious components of the psyche (egos or selves). They
do not allow for the manifestation of anything higher within a
person than the basic consciousness. They can be referred to as
lunar bodies. They are phantom-like, not solid like a physical body
is. The almost classic portrayal of a person projecting and looking like a ghost-like figure is the portrayal of a projection with a
lunar body.

Lunar vs Solar
Bodies

123

To be able to investigate properly and to function properly in both the higher and inferior dimensions, a superior type of body is needed—one that is solid and allows for the proper rising of the kundalini in it. That type of body is known as a solar body; it has a radiance and is firm to the touch. It's not vague like a lunar body. These solar bodies are the "bridal garments" or the "wedding dress of the soul," referred to in early Christianity, and the "bodies of gold" in ancient Egypt.

A body in the higher dimensions is not created by things like concentration, visualization, psychological observation, meditation, etc., but like all life it is born through sex—sexual alchemy to be exact. Sex is the creative force; all energy is ultimately sexual. Whoever really wants to understand the mysteries of life has to understand the mysteries of sex.

Solar bodies can be created for the different dimensions. Lunar bodies of the fifth dimension are replaced with solar ones—these allow the manifestation of superior spiritual parts within the psyche, which normally a person doesn't have.

In the fifth dimension a solar astral body allows the feeling of higher, more spiritual emotions, and a solar mental body allows the capacity to instantaneously comprehend without the entanglements of the ordinary mind. In the sixth dimension a solar body allows for the manifestation of the human soul. A solar body in the seventh dimension allows the manifestation of the spirit in its male and female aspects.

A few people are born with solar astral and mental bodies that were created in past times, but most have lunar bodies and will need to create solar ones if they want to have advanced spiritual development. There are also higher bodies than the solar ones, and solar bodies are replaced with them (golden bodies) with greater spiritual advancement. Golden bodies allow for the higher spiritual parts of the Being to be incarnated into human consciousness—the Father, Mother, and Son.

When exploring the astral plane, the psyche needs to be explored too. The astral world and dreams cannot be taken in isolation as something separate from the study of self-knowledge. Indeed, the astral world and self-knowledge cannot be taken as a complete study without including alchemy and esoteric knowledge, because the latter are indispensable for profound and in-depth astral experiences.

CHAPTER ELEVEN

BAD DREAMS, NIGHTMARES, AND SINISTER ENTITIES

A significant number of people who have an out-of-body experience see figures that appear dark and evil, or go to places that feel unpleasant. Another smaller yet still significant number (around 10 percent) of people who have near-death experiences report having a negative experience. Dreams can also be full of unpleasant experiences and situations of one kind or another.

BAD DREAMS

A large percentage of the population suffers from having more unpleasant dreams than pleasant ones; they include violence, being chased, trapped, fighting, falling, etc. These go on a sliding scale from bad dreams to horrific nightmares. They are usually more the reflection of the state of the psyche in the lower astral plane where most dreams occur than true nightmares. It's not surprising that many dreams are of these unpleasant, violent events if we look at some of the negative states that are experienced during daily life. We find anger, stress, fears of all kinds, hatred, and violence occurring everywhere, but what may be more surprising is that these low states can be voluntarily or subconsciously indulged in and even enjoyed. Think how popular amusement park rides are for example, where the overriding emotion is fear.

You only have to look at how many popular TV shows and movies contain violence, crime, and horror to see how much the feeling of the emotions evoked by them is enjoyed and sought after. It's also a self-perpetuating process, because the more that negative states are fed during the day, the stronger they become, and then the more the subconscious looks to feed them, and then the more they turn into bad dreams at night. Children who watch scary movies for example have in studies been found to be three times more likely to have nightmares that night than children who don't. With adults these states become stronger and more deeply entrenched.

The psyche is just continuing its activity from day to night, from wakefulness to dreams. Negative states that are in the psyche during the day continue to exist at night in dreams, but they emerge without the reality of the physical world to keep them in check. Then in dreams all those images and emotions that are part of the psyche become real events, projected from the subconscious. The psyche in the dream world can get reduced to its raw state where the most basic animalistic instincts and emotions are let loose, shaped by the model of the world created from the subconscious.

NIGHTMARES   *need a solar body*

True nightmares have a different kind of feel to them than the milder bad dreams and they tend to be more horrific. They occur when the dreamer goes right into the infra-dimensions instead of the usual lower astral plane. Eating a large meal before sleeping, and more importantly having an upset stomach increases the likelihood of nightmares occurring.

There is an energy that goes from the coccyx bone into the inferior dimensions which has a negative effect upon the human psyche and which drags or pulls the psyche downward; this energy is represented in mythology by demonic figures with tails, or as the descending serpent. These inferior dimensions are known as the Abyss or hell in different religions. It can be more difficult to get there to explore it because we need at least a solar astral body to enter it consciously. Some people who do not have solar bodies, although having many out-of-body experiences, are unable to find the Abyss and therefore conclude that it doesn't exist. Unless they wish to build their solar bodies through alchemy, they will remain stuck in their investigations.

The Abyss is experienced without self-awareness in nightmares, but we can go there to explore the darkness both within and without. Sometimes in the astral plane you can notice a kind of an opening that looks like a mouth or a slit in the fabric of space itself. This is the entrance or portal between the astral plane and the inferior dimensions. It has been known in the Western world as the mouth of hell since early Christian times.

Some people who've had near-death experiences recall walking down a corridor and getting to some kind of gate or barrier. Some are turned back at this point and go back to their bodies. Whereas in positive NDEs the light at the end of the tunnel passes from the fifth dimension to a higher one, in hellish NDEs, the mouth of hell, the corridor, and the gates are a passageway to the inferior dimensions. At the gates are the toll collectors mentioned in early esoteric Christianity, and nearby are the waiting rooms, where some who recall NDEs say they were asked to go back to earth as their time was not yet up. Many others recall passing through or being swallowed by the jaws of a crocodile, represented in ancient Egypt by the female deity Ammit. The female deity Kali has a similar role in Hinduism, and in the Pistis Sophia, an ancient esoteric Christian text, Jesus explains how the soul of a sinner is taken down into hell before the mother goddess Persephone for punishment.

It's interesting for the astral explorer to see things like this while out of the body and later to go and read about them in ancient texts.

It's possible to stop having nightmares if you eliminate the parts within your psychology that cause them and have other spiritual parts instead—then it's possible to go to paradisiacal places.

True nightmares require quite a lot more explanation than I can give here.

SINISTER PRESENCES AND PLACES

From what I've seen, pretty much everyone who has a high enough number of out-of-body experiences will have some negative ones. In a similar way, there are many dreams containing unpleasant scenes and even nightmares. In dreams, much of this is due to the content and structure of the psyche, which is full of fears, aggression, etc. In conscious out-of-body experiences however, while the negative parts of the psyche do have their impact, there are other factors at work too.

It's important to realize that not everything we encounter in the astral plane is benevolent; not everyone is benevolent here in daily life either, and we would be wrong to go around in day-to-day life with the illusion that everyone and everything is wonderful and loving all the time. Therefore, it's worth understanding what you find in the astral plane, both good and bad, positive and negative; in this way you can be prepared for what you come across.

To get a wider picture of the dark side of the astral plane I recommend that you study more esoteric work, but I'll explain a little about the malevolent forces that you will at some time inevitably face there.

In most religions and myths of ancient times we find the struggle of opposites, light and darkness, positive and negative, etc. It's part of the structure of the way that life is created that opposites exist and it is necessary for life to exist; it is also necessary for learning and spiritual growth. If we were to exist in light alone, we would have no knowledge even of our own existence. It is the struggle against the darkness that makes us strong and gives us knowledge.

This duality and opposites also exists in the fifth dimension, so negative things can be experienced in dreams or when consciously in the astral plane.

Just as there are spiritual beings, so too are there beings who are the opposite—negative beings. The beings that are spiritual are that way because they have created themselves to be so. The same applies to the negative beings; they have transformed themselves into creatures of darkness. It is possible to awaken in light, for which the darkness within (the egos, the different elements of the subconscious) must be overcome and the forces of darkness outside must be defeated in their attempt to stop one from awakening. They inevitably come to try to stop anyone who takes up the spiritual work seriously.

You may have seen beings of darkness in nightmares or in dreams; many people when astral projecting have met them or have sensed their presence, regardless of whether they had any religious convictions or not.

Demons are frequently represented in different religions throughout the world. They are beings that have awakened in evil, or beings of light who have fallen, and they belong to a hierarchical structure that's organized according to the level of awakened evil consciousness each of them has. We find them in the astral and mental planes of the fifth dimension, although they reside in the inferior dimensions and enter the astral and mental planes.

There is much to learn from darkness as it is light in its opposite and is a substance. Much of that learning, however, is more advanced than simply learning to astral project and being prepared to deal with any dark figures that you may find in the astral plane. So for people starting out, it's important to learn to deal with fear when coming across a sinister being or situation in the astral plane—it's worth remembering that they don't so much cause harm physically as harm spiritual development. For example, when you get to the astral there may be some waiting there for you to frighten you so that you fly back to your body, or to distract you so that you don't go somewhere more spiritual or discover what you need to.

To the unwary they use deceit; they can say things that are misleading and can easily fool someone into taking their advice, which inevitably is harmful for the real spiritual work. They can even appear as one's idea of holy beings, preaching about love, etc., but their real purpose is to take people away from objective study and the spiritual path.

They can stir up ego states, both in the astral plane and in daily life, inflaming passions and desires and leading one astray. They can cause the astral world to look unclear or darkened. They can make an initiate fall and can do works on the astral body so that the kundalini, an essential aspect of the spiritual path, does not rise, rendering the body disabled for the esoteric work.

There are many cases in history and folklore of these beings. One very well recorded type of encounter happens when a person is partly in the astral, lying in bed, and feels totally paralyzed (this kind of sleep paralysis is a normal function that prevents sleepwalking), sensing or seeing a fiendish figure close by or actually in contact with them. Although the subconscious can create a vision of a sinister entity out of fear and imagination, or a physical person in the room can take on a demonic presence through the subconscious, experience shows that unhallowed beings can and do take advantage of that natural time when we're not quite in the physical body and not quite detached in the astral body and so are unable to move.

THE NIGHTMARE, BY HENRY FUSELI, 1781.

In times like this, as long as you are conscious, you can use what are called recitations of protection, which are words that have the power to expel evil beings and return them back to their abode or disable them.

Many people have been deceived by sinister figures. In the astral plane you can call spiritual beings and get help and teachings from them, but often if you call, a malign being will arrive that looks exactly like the spiritual being you are calling, so use a protective recitation if you need to. If the being is evil it will go; if it is the real one, it will stay. You can also use your intuition, because sometimes you can tell an evil being just by looking at it, particularly if you look into its eyes, which can look dark and evil.

If you are negative toward someone, your own subconscious can make them appear as an evil figure to you in a dream or the astral plane. In that case your own negativity may persuade you that it was real. This is another reason to work to get your psyche as clear and objective as possible.

If you feel you need some assistance you could ask for help from your Being; the Father is most appropriate. I've encountered so many negative entities while out of the body. They come again and again in many different guises. Sometimes they appeared in confusing ways, such as when I saw a spiritual teacher, or what looked like him, and he started telling me something. However, as he spoke, my intuition told me that there was something wrong. So I stared closely into his eyes, and as I did, they appeared blackish and dark with an evil resonance about them. I immediately knew that it wasn't him but a negative entity, a being from the other side in disguise. Deceit is a major weapon of the forces of evil.

EXPERIENCES IN INFERIOR REGIONS

Not all experiences of darkness are of simple scary beings in dreams; there is much to learn of realities of the inferior regions that is essential for the understanding of life and death. Traveling consciously out of the body and exploring the inferior regions is different to involuntarily having nightmares, and it gives access to knowledge that is otherwise hidden. Nightmares happen due to the low state of the psyche, but from the astral plane you can go into the region that is their source to explore the nature of darkness. To successfully explore there though, you will need to have created a solar astral body.

There are some entities from the dark side that are very complex. One night out of my body I traveled through dark regions of hell and there I saw a figure dressed in black. He had with him an entourage who followed him; this entourage has its counterpart amongst a certain group of people in the physical world who are obviously under the influence of the dark side and wear black as well. They were in front of me and approached me. I also walked toward them. The leading figure who seemed larger than the others had a somewhat distinguished appearance, like a middle-aged person with a high responsibility. I had my sword and the recitations to expel demons, but he walked toward me and I walked toward him; each of us were in the other's way. We stopped right in front of each other as though a conflict were about to begin and I asked him who he was—he replied "Bael." He looked closely at me and I looked at him. I looked straight into his eyes and to my astonishment I saw evil, but not evil of the other grotesque beings I had previously encountered, but a great, deep, sublime evil intelligence.

It was an intelligence that was dark and yet was vast. His eyes were portals into a deep blackness, so deep they seemed to encompass all the darkness. And, as I looked in, the darkness looked back at me and he looked at me; he looked at me and through me, like he saw something more than eyes could see. I moved to one side and let him pass, as though we knew that to fight each other would have been in neither of our interests. He and his entourage kept walking along that road, disappearing into the foggy darkness.

When I was learning about the basics of astral projection I was with a group of people practicing a meditation exercise called a koan, which is a question that doesn't have an answer. If you keep asking this kind of question, eventually the mind, when trying to find an answer where there is none, will become completely silent and then you'll have an out-of-body experience to a spiritual dimension.

The koan was called the hanging man. We had to imagine that we were hanging over the edge of a cliff with our hands and legs tied, holding onto a rope with our teeth, and we had to work out how to get out of that situation.

I lay down to sleep and concentrated on the koan. As I concentrated, sleep came over me and I held my concentration. Suddenly I was out of my body and the visualization of hanging from a rope somehow took a completely new turn; there was no rope and no cliff, but I was suspended in hell. I felt what it was to lose that last opportunity which we have in a human life and to be thrown into the Abyss.

That rope represented a tiny thread of hope that kept me from being in that terrible situation. I could feel exactly how it felt to be condemned to hell, the bitter desperation which no words can describe. The tiny thread of hope was the repentance and asking to one's Being. My situation was also humanity's situation, ready to fall into the Abyss, an inescapable fate were it not for that minute opportunity—the intervention of the supernatural force of the Being.

My pleas and laments to get me out of there had a deeper meaning than simply getting me away from the place I was in—they were a desperate cry for help to escape my fate. Suddenly I found myself above my body and could see the ceiling above me, my body was below, and soon after I merged back into my body and got up in the physical world. I understood that koan had a deeper and more profound meaning—it indicated the state of humanity.

THROUGH THE MOUTH OF HELL

One night when consciously out of my body in the astral plane, I walked down a street near my old high school. I looked up and saw a kind of a gap in the sky; it was a gap in space itself, and intuitively I felt that I should explore it, so I rose into the air. Then, as I got close, I could see demons guarding it on the outside; they had that classical demonic appearance. I expelled them with a recitation and went into this slit which was like a mouth. It was dark inside, even though it was nighttime and dark outside.

As I went in, I was in a corridor that sloped downward. I walked down it and walking with me were the deceased. They came through continuously, just walking in the one direction with no

THE GARDEN OF EARTHLY DELIGHTS, INNER RIGHT WING (HELL), BY HIERONYMUS BOSCH, 1504.

notion to walk in any other direction and no notion to communicate with each other.

Eventually I came to a series of tollgates or booths. Each person went to a booth; someone stood at each booth and collected something from each person. As the deceased passed through the tollgate they kept a human form but inside were animals, just animals enjoying the resonance and feel of the egos. They vibrated with them making growls and groans as they walked from the toll area into the darkness beyond. They had given up to the toll collector what it was to be human, as it had only been given for a short time—they passed through the gates as animals.

I also passed through a tollgate but gave up nothing, and instead of walking into the entrance of the area of darkness, I went into one of several waiting rooms to the right. The light was strange and subdued and I felt the fear of being in that place. I knew that I was being shown my fate and humanity's fate at the same time, and I knew who could help me in that moment, the Being who out of love helps to bring souls up out of that abysmal place to give them another human life and another opportunity—Judas. He was not a villain, but actually a good disciple who performed a role for Jesus—as the recently discovered Gospel of Judas shows.

I called his name over and over and he came through the door. He was such an unimposing figure who irradiated a quiet kind of warmth, the sort that would pass unnoticed in the world. He said to me, "You have to practice, whether you like it or not." I responded with silence—a silence that communicated a reply, "Yes, I have to." Soon after that I came back to my body; I knew that I had to do what I'd been told.

Years later I spoke to a woman who had a near-death experience; in it, she passed through the jaws of a crocodile and found herself in a waiting room with other people. Someone came in and told her that she had to go back because it wasn't her time yet. You can see that crocodile represented in many Egyptian paintings, which in the depictions is there to swallow up those who are to enter hell.

Also years later I came across medieval woodcut illustrations depicting what I had seen in the mouth of hell and discovered a mention of the toll collectors in a Nag Hammadi Library text. I obviously wasn't the first to travel there and come back. Later still, the discovery of the Gospel of Judas was made public.

DETAIL FROM THE PAINTING SECOND COMING, DEPICTING THE MOUTH OF HELL, BY GEORGIOS KLONTZAS, FROM THE LATE 16TH CENTURY

PROTECTION AGAINST SINISTER ENTITIES

Just as here we have to protect ourselves, our belongings, our homes, and so on, we also have to protect ourselves against sinister entities in the astral plane, and we can do that by using recitations of protection, which are words that expel them.

Recitations of protection have been used throughout history and references can be found in many esoteric texts. These phrases have the power to return sinister entities back to their abode or to disable them, and lots of people have used them with great success. So it's worth experimenting and seeing how they work—unless you try them, there's no way you are going to know of their effectiveness.

Whenever you see a sinister figure in the astral plane, or a being that you are unsure of, or if you go into the astral world and it's dark, or in daily life if you sense a negative vibe or presence, or before going to sleep, you can use a recitation. They work best when done strongly with a lot of conviction and when your psychic energies are strong.

There are various formulas that have been recommended as recitations for this purpose; some recommend saying the Lord's Prayer to ward off evil forces and beings, but I haven't tried it. Two that I have used and found very effective are "Jupiter" and "Bellilin." I learnt "Jupiter" from the work of my former teacher Rabolu and "Bellilin" from the work of his teacher Samael Aun Weor. You'll need to be open minded to try them.

THE RECITATION OF THE COSMIC FATHER

This is known as the recitation of Jupiter. It's a request to the male aspect of the male/female divinity to assist us to expel negative entities.

Jupiter is a name used in history by the Romans for the Cosmic Father; it is basically the same as the Christian Father, the Etruscan Tinia, the Hindu Indra, or the Greek Zeus amongst many others. Using any of the names will be fine, but Jupiter is the tried and tested one.

> To do this recitation, place your left hand over your solar plexus, which is around the navel. This protects against sinister forces while the recitation is being pronounced.

Put the fingers of your right hand in the shape of a gun with the palm facing down, extend the index and middle fingers, close the other two fingers and extend the thumb outward.

Extend your arm straight in front of you, pointing at the entity if you see one, and then pronounce the following words three times:

In the Name of Jupiter, Father of Deities,
I expel you, Te Vigos Cosilim.

If you are in the astral plane, you can sometimes see rays coming out of your hand. You could imagine the rays as you do it in the physical world. Te Vigos Cosilim (pronounced "Teh Veegoss Cossileem") doesn't have a literal translation, but the mantra's words are effective in dispelling sinister entities.

You can listen to a sound file of this recitation on my website.

BELLILIN

Bellilin is a divine wind that casts away evil and negativity. It's particularly useful if for some reason you cannot move or cannot put your hands into position for the recitation of Jupiter.

You don't need to do anything with your arms, it's sung, and you can use the sound file on my website as a guide to learn it.

Pay particular attention to the tone of it so that you pronounce it correctly.

You need to say any recitation of protection all the way through three times for it to be fully effective.

Here are the words. You pronounce it three times:

Bellilin Bellilin Bellilin,
Amphora of salvation,
I would like to be next to you,
Materialism has no strength next to me,
Bellilin Bellilin Bellilin.

Amphora means a container, but in this context it's one of a spiritual nature.

There's no need to be frightened if the figure is still there while you are still pronouncing the recitation, although it can sometimes disappear once you begin. If it is there while you're doing it, continue and the recitation will be effective as soon as you complete saying it.

If for any reason you come across something and you are not sure whether it is from the good or evil side, use a recitation to check. If it's good it will stay; if it's bad it will usually go or be disabled.

Many people have been deceived by sinister entities, so if in doubt, use a recitation of protection. But also use your intuition, because sometimes you can tell an evil being just by looking at it, particularly if you look into its eyes, which can look dark and evil.

SOME EXAMPLES OF RECITATIONS AGAINST SINISTER FIGURES

I've used recitations effectively for many years. One time, a horrible animal attacked me in the astral plane; as soon as I saw it I began to use Jupiter, because it's faster than Bellilin. It started running at me and bit me on the arm, even though I was expelling it. I continued my recitation but the animal stayed there. It only left when I had finished saying the recitation the three times needed to complete it.

Many times I have been met by a demonic being who took the form of a spiritual guide in order to deceive me, but you can learn to tell what they really are just by looking into their eyes. If you see that they are evil, expel them.

Years ago I met some people who appeared to be very spiritual and who impressed me with their ability to astral project at will every night. They had amazing psychic faculties, but I noticed they performed symbolic gestures the opposite way to the ones I did, that is, they performed them as do those who are of darkness and used inverted symbols.

They gave me an object just before I drove home one evening and I put it in the back of the car. As I was driving in the dark along a country lane, what appeared to be a strange looking animal jumped onto the road in front of me, I swerved the car, and the animal scampered to the side of the road and vanished—disappeared that is. I took the object out of the back of the car and threw it away; things didn't look good.

One night in the astral plane I saw one of them doing a work on my spine, where the kundalini rises, and inserting things into my kidneys that blocked the flow of energy. After this, a spiritual being appeared to me in the astral plane and gave me a plant which is used for protection. Then I asked the beings of light to undo what the negative ones had done to me. I performed a ritual with a group of people to break their sinister influence and it worked.

I never saw them after that, although some months later I met one of them again in the astral plane. This time however, I commanded him to reveal himself to me. He lifted into the air, turned into a grotesque demon and disappeared into the darkness from where he came.

These were people who had awakened their consciousness for evil, but thanks to the protection of the beings of light, they didn't harm me or anyone around me. They were however, infiltrating an esoteric society; darkness likes to do that sort of thing.

You can also use the recitations of protection at night before you go to sleep, so that you clear away any dark beings or forces that might be there or might appear during the night. And if you think you're stronger than negative entities and have no need for recitations, you will be easily deceived by them.

AN OLD DEPICTION OF A CIRCLE OF PROTECTION. THE ASTROLOGER OF
THE NINETEENTH CENTURY, BY ROBERT CROSS (RAPHAEL) SMITH, 1825.

THE CIRCLE OF PROTECTION

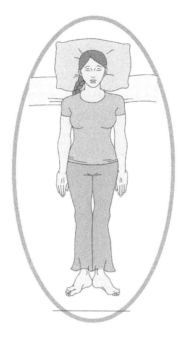

When the environment is cleared of negative forces with a recitation of protection, the area needs to be protected and sealed so that they, or other negative forces, cannot come back in straight away. For this, a protective circle is needed. This is a circle of light that is held by the elementals of nature, which forms a barrier that stops any evil being from entering. It is drawn in a circle using imagination and doing a work with the elementals of nature, which makes the circle strong and sustains it.

Elementals of nature are essences (the raw consciousnesses) of creatures that are evolving. They have been known throughout history in various myths and legends as fairies, pixies, gnomes, salamanders, sylphs, etc.

Many ancient peoples knew how to work with these elementals of nature; they are the same ones that we use for this circle.

Having expelled the dark entity using a recitation, then you draw a circle to seal entities out.

In order to do it, you say the following words:

> *My Father, please order my elemental intercessor to wrap a magical circle of protection around me [or the bed or the room or whatever you choose], so that no evil entity can harm me.*

As you are saying the above you imagine a circle formed by a beam of light being drawn around wherever you have chosen.

It may help to extend your right arm and point with your index finger where you want the circle to be drawn as you are imagining it.

The Father is the male aspect of each one's own Being. We ask that part of the Being because he has the power to do it.

You do this three times making sure that the circle is joined and complete.

This can be done before going to bed at night, or at any time that you feel you need to do it. Then once it's done, no evil entity can get in. The circle stays until you move out of it physically. When you move out of it physically, you break it.

Jesus used a circle of protection when he protected a woman who was about to be stoned. He drew a circle in the sand around her and she was saved.

Some years ago someone I taught this to was a bit skeptical about this, but nevertheless he drew the circle around himself before going to sleep. He woke up in the astral plane to find himself unable to move, with an evil-looking cat in front of him. He became frightened and started spitting at the cat, because that was all he thought he could do. Then he noticed that he had a circle of light around him and that the cat could not get in. He then woke up, back in his body. He should have practiced the recitation of Bellilin more because he could have used it to make the cat disappear.

The more that you practice these recitations, the more you will remember to use them and remember the words to them in the astral world. You can also find yourself using them in your dreams if you practice them enough. Listen carefully to the sound files and repeat them over and over again until you have learnt them by heart. It's important to memorize them fluently so you'll be far more likely to use them in the astral plane. It won't help if you're before a sinister creature in the astral plane and can't remember all the words.

If you go into the astral plane a few times, you may be surprised how quickly you need to use these techniques; once you do use them, you'll see just how effective they are and you'll realize that you are able to deal with malign forces and are able to move around in the astral plane and get teachings unhindered by them.

USEFUL TIPS WHEN USING THE RECITATIONS AND THE CIRCLE OF PROTECTION

∞ If a sinister entity tries to frighten you as you are coming out of your body, right in the moment of projection or during the sleep paralysis, it's best not to move or try to end the exercise out of fear. Rather, you should behave as though you haven't heard or seen anything, and without worrying or moving, sing the recitation of Bellilin to get rid of it.

∞ If you're not sure whether you've drawn the circle of protection well, start again. If you need to start the recitations from the beginning, do so.

∞ If you're expelling a sinister entity or figure and it begins to mock your recitation, it's trying to undermine your confidence, so be focused when you're saying it.

QUESTIONS AND ANSWERS

Are there also other ways of dealing with sinister figures besides the recitations and circle? I have heard that if you mention Jesus' name these figures disappear.

Pronouncing a spiritual being's name is not a reliable way of getting rid of them. You will find it more effective to use one of the recitations rather than using the name of a spiritual being. Fiendish entities can even appear in disguise when you invoke a spiritual being in the astral plane.

While creating the circle of protection, do I also have to say the statement three times or is only the circle to be created three times?

You have to say the statement three times and draw the circle three times as well.

I understand that negative forces not only affect us in the astral world, but in daily life too. Can we use a recitation and the circle of protection in the physical plane also to keep dark forces away?

Yes, you can also use the recitations and circle of protection in daily life to keep negative entities away if you feel you need to.

Will the circle of protection keep dark forces away from only me, or will it protect all the persons I work with?

The circle can protect everyone inside it as long as no one goes in or out of it and breaks it.

Can I create a circle of protection for others even if I am not in the circle? If I can, what will be the statement?

Yes, you can draw it around others even if you are not in it. You say everything the same as when you draw it around yourself except that instead of asking for it to be drawn around yourself, you ask for it to be drawn around the people.

Since my Lord is Christ (not the lesser god Jupiter), how am I going to protect myself when I astral travel? I cannot, therefore, invoke Jupiter for protection because I don't believe in lesser gods. Can I invoke Christ for protection instead?

Jupiter is another name for the "Father" and he is very important in Christianity. These are just names for the same thing; it's not worth getting stuck over them. If you stick to the rigid confines of a fixed point of view you will not be able to explore. If you want to explore the unknown you have to ask yourself what you really know about it and whether you only want to believe in something, because experience is needed to discover the truth. If you try this recitation you will see that it works. In Christianity the Christ is different from the Father, and the Christ would itself repel any sinister force, but this is a specific recitation that appeals to the Father. If you are really stuck you could try the Lord's Prayer, because if you don't want to pronounce anything outside what you are comfortable with, you have nothing to lose by reciting it.

Every night before I sleep I use a recitation of protection for the house and ask for a circle of protection around the entire house. Although I have not knowingly experienced anything that would indicate I needed to protect my house in this manner before now, I try to be diligent and practice what I'm learning. After forgetting to do a recitation of protection and draw the circle one night, everything you said came true and I have no hesitation in heeding every word of advice offered on this subject! As I said, I have never knowingly been troubled by sinister forces before, but it seems that now they know what I'm up to, they really are out to annoy me!

Yes, they really are there. There is a huge war going on between the forces of light and darkness. Most of this is unknown to the average person, who probably feels they have no need for protection.

I was just wondering whether these are things that must be said aloud, or may be said silently in the mind?

Say them aloud, because the word has strength and because then you'll do it aloud in a dream or in the astral plane too and it has more power there. It depends on the situation in daily life though, because there are many times when you have to pronounce it silently.

Are some of these negative entities created by us from negative habits like negative thinking?

Some figures in dreams or in the astral plane are just projections of the subconscious or are cases of the imagination becoming a false reality. So it's important to study how the subconscious works so that you are able to discriminate properly and are able to see what is actually there. However, there are also beings that have awakened in evil.

As the mind creates in the astral plane, some unpleasant things we may encounter over there are created by people—these are known as astral larvae. They predominate in places where there is a lot of emotion, where egos predominate, for example in a room where there has been a lot of anger, lust, or drunkenness. These larvae harm the astral body.

There are also ones that are created by sexual desires, which are commonly known as incubi or succubi. They have an existence outside of the individual, as they are essentially highly developed egos and come and go into someone. They can be destroyed with an alchemical work.

There are also the parts of the subconscious that affect OBEs; these are various ego states such as anger, pride, fear, and the rest of the many facets of the subconscious. They can also take forms which are encountered in dreams and astral experiences.

When you dream about a negative creature, does that mean that in the astral there is an evil being that is working on you? I had a dream about a vampire bat and it flew down and bit me on the left shoulder. It felt so real and I couldn't get it off of me. I woke up and my shoulder felt funny. Was something doing me harm in the astral and I just didn't realize I was in the astral?

Yes, it could have been; they do attack at night like that and bats in the astral plane can also have associations with sinister occultism. You should use your intuition to try to work out its source; animals attacking can also symbolize egos or enemies that are attacking.

As I lay in bed, right before the astral split, in the moment of paralysis, a form descended on me in my bed. I fought out of fear at first and tried to fight it off, but I felt nothing there. Then finally I felt an arm wrap around me and I touched it (in my astral body). It was not threatening, but benign. Last night I lay upon the couch and drifted off. At the moment of the split, and paralysis, I felt an animal that seemed like a cat jump upon the couch and lay upon me. I tried out of fear to smack it away but nothing was there, only making myself move to regain bodily control. This repeated over and over until I let the fear go and then I could feel it. I was feeling it with my astral arms, not the physical ones. I'm learning how our astral bodies are different from our physical ones, and that we don't move them the same way. I am learning, albeit in small steps, but the most amazing thing about it is that someone is helping me, and showing me things. I'm slowly but surely going down a new road and I'm growing into much more than I was before.

It could have been your subconscious, but there are infernal beings that use that very common stage of astral experience known as sleep paralysis to frighten people and put them off the astral world and esoteric knowledge. They sometimes take the shape of animals; it could be this is what you're seeing.

Having the right tools is enabling me to observe aspects of fear and have the potential to deal effectively with each issue that arises. I feel that ultimately there isn't actually anything to fear—it's just a matter of proving it to myself, which gives me solid confidence.
In your experience, is an individual's level of spiritual development likely to be tested to the same degree by evil forces?

The more we progress spiritually, the more the infernal forces attack us and try to stop us. They see us then as people who are getting away from their grip and who begin to pose a threat to them.

The further into the light we go, the more the darkness comes against us. How we face it can be used by spiritual beings to measure our spiritual development.

I had a strange experience last night while asleep. I woke up suddenly after a vision of a rock band in black. I recognized one of the people in it from the past. I woke up feeling I was being shown negative beings. It felt like it was connected to my questioning at the moment regarding negative beings. I still find it difficult to differentiate whether it has come from my own subconscious or from the astral world. Should I be going with the initial feelings when I wake up? I have found several times in this course that I have my questions answered in dreams. Is this a reliable source? Is it common?

It's usually best to go with the initial feeling you had when you woke up, but if in doubt, keep an open mind about it. Information is given through dreams so you'll need to be able to differentiate between those and projections from the subconscious. It can take some time to learn and change enough to be able to regularly distinguish between different kinds of astral experiences—the ability improves as you develop spiritually.

Answers to problems are quite common in dreams; that is where you can get teachings directly from spiritual beings. If you can keep learning, you will keep getting taught.

Can other beings within the astral plane sever the silver cord?

The cord is severed by divine beings when the appointed moment of death arrives.

Is there any chance that someone or something else could get into my physical body while I'm off traveling in my astral body?

No, there is no danger of that happening. You are attached to your own physical body by the silver cord, so only you can get in. Also, there is no danger because you are in the astral plane every night when you go to bed and sleep and you always wake up fine in the morning. That is, unless you decide to become a medium or a channeler, which I don't recommend, since when doing that all kinds of things can get in without you knowing.

Whenever I have a nightmare I always prove to myself in the dream that, "It's only a dream—nothing to worry about." At that point the dream either ends or I gain control of it for a while and it ends soon. What does this mean?

Whenever you have a true nightmare, it's less likely that you will remember that it's a dream while you're having one. Nightmares are different kinds of dreams with sinister or horrific things in them; they have quite a different flavor. In the dreams where you had control, even bad dreams with unpleasant characters in them, etc., you were partially awake there. So if you are in a dream and you know that it's a dream, say to yourself that you are in the astral world and jump with the intention of flying. You will see that you can fly and can then travel to different places.

I was aware that I was in bed, but I was also sitting at the foot of the bed and a being swathed in black (very deep black) came in the room. At first I was rather interested, then fear took over and as it approached me I started to fight it. I remember while doing this, I could not move my real body. I continued to fight and try to speak, but was paralyzed. I finally woke up. This scared me quite a bit. Has anyone else had an experience like this?

Experiences like this are quite common and are well recorded in history. You were paralyzed because you were in the transition period between being awake and asleep, and so did not have movement of the physical body.

Although the subconscious can imagine a lot in those circumstances, it is also possible that what you perceived coming toward you was a sinister figure from the lower astral world taking advantage of your lack of movement.

There's nothing to be frightened about though. They can be there at any time; it's just that you were aware of its presence then. Use a recitation to get rid of anything like that.

I find if I come out of a dream that I don't want to leave, I just remain still. If I just had a nightmare and don't want to fall asleep into it again, I change body positions.

By remaining still the astral body has not yet locked into the physical body, and so you can go back into the dream you just had before you woke up more easily. By moving you wake up properly, and then you're much less likely to go back into the dream you had before you woke. This applies whether it is a normal dream or a nightmare.

In any case, you are likely to move as soon as you wake up from a nightmare because of the fright. Nightmares are different from normal dreams and they occur in a different place.

It's possible to avoid recurring nightmares, and if you do an inner work based on the right spiritual principles, you may eventually be able to prevent them altogether.

A tip to avoid the likelihood of having nightmares is to avoid having a large meal or anything that can unsettle the stomach before you go to sleep.

It's also worth knowing that taking consciousness-altering drugs increases the chance of having nightmares.

CHAPTER TWELVE

SCIENTIFIC PROOF
FOR OUT-OF-BODY
EXPERIENCES

SCIENCE CANNOT PROVE OR DISPROVE what occurs in out-of-body experiences, as the technology available is not sufficiently advanced to be able to do that. It would be supportive to many starting out in traveling beyond the body to have some kind of verification from the scientific establishment that it is real and perfectly alright to do, but you can't get that kind of absolute verification from science. You can only really understand astral travel by personally having out-of-body experiences and then you are only able to talk on level terms with people who have actually done it.

THE INADEQUACY OF SCIENTIFIC METHODS

There have been experiments carried out by scientists to verify whether out-of-body experiences are real or whether they are a figment of the imagination; while travelers have provided many compelling accounts that could only have been experienced while out of the body, none provide conventional science with the kind of proof that most are looking for, which will give it universal acceptance, and I doubt they will find it.

This is because of the scientific methods used to verify whether something is real or not. The methods require that evidence is acquired from phenomena that are external to the researcher and that the evidence is verifiable by others.

This poses problems for science when it comes to astral travel, as the subject (the traveler) when experiencing the astral is in another dimension, which is subject to different laws. The subject may go to a place in the astral plane, but the scientist has no evidence from the three-dimensional world that they have actually traveled anywhere, apart from the accounts of the subject. All a researcher would see is that the subject slept, and has to rely upon their account of what happened. Even if more than one person in the experiment meets in a place in the astral plane, a scientist only has two or more accounts of traveling and no actual physical evidence apart from the accounts of sleeping people.

Science is not sufficiently advanced enough that it can look at brain waves or other bodily functions and tell what people are experiencing during an OBE. I spoke to a woman recently who was seriously ill in hospital and close to death—she had an out-of-body experience (not technically a near-death one as her body hadn't died) and described how while bodily unconscious she left her body, hovered slightly above the ground, looked around the room, could see medical staff around her, was able to read her medical notes, and recalled how a doctor came into the room wearing a red turban. When revived she accurately described the events that had taken place in the room while she was unconscious. The notes she described turned out to be accurate and staff were perplexed about her account of the doctor in the red turban as he was not the usual doctor and had only visited that day to fill in for an absent member of staff—she was completely unconscious during the whole time of that doctor's visit and had no prior knowledge of it.

Conventional science, lacking the means to study while actually in the fifth dimension, can offer little of worth to those seeking answers to understand situations and experiences like this; to find answers an individual needs to explore out of the body personally. This is why I refer to astral travel as an inner science; it is repeatedly verifiable to the person who actually does it.

ANECDOTAL EVIDENCE AND TESTS

There has been enough anecdotal information given from subjects to show that the simplest explanation—that consciousness does leave the body and travel outside of it—is not irrefutable in current academic terms, and that the accounts of traveling, seeing distant objects, places, and events that actually exist while the physical body was asleep may, theoretically in some cases, be what they say they are. Yet many inept theories such as the effects of hormones, hallucinations, or the stimulation of various parts of the brain continue to be thought up by scientists and academics to explain what the subjects who claim to travel to distant places out of their bodies are actually experiencing. These ideas become even less credible in the light of near-death experiences, which frequently take place when the body is technically dead and the brain is unable to function.

How many scientists actually think of exploring out-of-body experiences by having these experiences themselves? Once you do, you get into the realms of inner esoteric science, and conventional science won't go there.

A few try (and some have tried inconclusively) to provide scientific evidence of consciousness existing outside the body by performing tests where the subject tries to project and see an object, color, or number placed out of physical sight by the experimenter, and then recount the color or number, etc., they saw whilst out of the body once they wake up physically. This is possible to do, however, the astral plane, being under different laws to this dimension, can give unexpected results for the traveler—the object may not be there or the subject could find themselves in a changed environment. Applying the laws of the third dimension to those of the fifth is completely inadequate.

THE PROBLEMS WITH THE SUBJECTIVE NATURE OF THE PSYCHE

Another problem is the subjective nature of the psyche. The subconscious affects the psyche in out-of-body experiences in ways that it does not here, with the result that many out-of-body experiences are subjective and not clear. Thoughts are a type of energy that condenses to form in the astral plane, so if for example you are thinking about being in a concert hall, it will become real for you and you will be in one (in the same way that you would in the dream state), even though it is not actually there. Should thoughts about eating ice cream appear, you can suddenly find yourself eating it, but it doesn't actually exist.

Therefore someone without the information from the five senses usually sees projections or a model of the world from their subconscious and not what is actually in the astral plane, or they may mix perceptions of the astral world with projections of their own subconscious and thus be unable to give a clear account of what is actually in that dimension. But the fact that some out-of-body experiences can be subjective does not mean that they all are—some experiences are clear and give results that could only be achieved if consciousness was separated from the body.

This is why the study of the psyche is vital in any exploration out of the body. A person must be able to have the psyche clear of its own projections to see what is real, and that requires an accurate study of the psyche. Subjects taking experiments for scientists have no real knowledge of the psyche and many have little experience of the astral plane; therefore, they are likely to give subjective results, which correspondingly lack scientific credibility. With clear out-of-body experiences however, if someone is in a place in the astral plane, they can give a clear account of it when they come back to this world, even relating things that would not have been possible for them to have seen from their sleeping body.

OBJECTIVE PERSONAL EXPERIENCE AS A MEANS TO EXPLORE OUT OF THE BODY

There are other factors to take into account that belong to the nature of life in the fifth dimension, and the practical way to discover those factors is through personal exploration in that dimension and a thorough study of self-knowledge. Even if the scientific experiment were to succeed according to its own criteria, many theories could be put forward to try to explain the results that do not include the whole person's consciousness being separate from the physical body.

While science uses current methodology, it is constrained in what it can discover of the fifth dimension: it wishes to apply three-dimensional laws to the fifth dimension without understanding what the laws of that dimension are. If you can personally explore outside the body in a clear way, then you can study the dimension that you're in to see what's there, to understand its laws, and how it operates. No one can do this from the third dimension.

Another factor to consider is that in an out-of-body experience, what is experienced is often due to the learning of the individual, and as anyone who explores out of the body sufficiently will have found, there are other life forms existing in that plane. There is more going on than meets the three-dimensional eye. The astral plane is used by beings who live there for the learning of those of us who are alive in this world. For scientists to factor that into the equation is far beyond their scope.

CHAPTER THIRTEEN

NEAR-DEATH
EXPERIENCES

NEAR-DEATH EXPERIENCES ARE ANOTHER WAY in which it is possible to experience existence outside the body. In a near-death experience, a person's body dies and their mind and consciousness continues to exist outside the body. Strictly speaking, according to the definition of the terminology it's not a pre-death experience or a post-revival one, but it takes place at the time when the body is actually dead and that usually means the brain is dead; in practice though, in many cases they do occur before actual physical death, usually in the preceding unconsciousness.

These kinds of experiences do have some differences to out-of-body experiences, notably in that the consciousness is no longer sending information back to the physical body via the silver cord, the brain no longer affects it, and there is no two-way body/consciousness process taking place. Life in the three-dimensional world in the body has ended, and the NDE experience is part of a wider process of death and moving on. This is why they tend to be clear experiences of that process, without so many of the projections and influences of the psyche, or of the experiences geared toward the learning of the individual which we get with OBEs; the time for correcting the psyche and for learning has ended and the experience is about moving on.

ASCENT OF THE BLESSED, BY
HIERONYMUS BOSCH. 1500-1504.

In an NDE, the deceased is beginning a journey that takes them to a future existence, determined by what they have done in life. They initially come out of their bodies into the astral plane, which normally appears just like the physical world.

NDEs are quite common and exist in all cultures around the world and happen to people of all ages. Statistical reports have said that around one in ten people who die and revive have an NDE. The figure is rising however, as more accounts are reported or recorded and as medical technology improves. There are even accounts given from children as young as three.

With conscious psychological activity present in the absence of brain function, NDEs show that consciousness can exist outside of brain function.

EXPERIENCES IN NDEs

It's worth watching or reading about people's accounts of their own near-death experiences, as I can only summarize some general trends here. Every person's is unique, although there are striking similar elements in them. Many people say they are conscious of being outside their body and experience floating out of the body and seeing what is happening around them. Many recall going through a dark tunnel with a light at the end of it, seeing pleasant landscapes, being in a spiritual place, and meeting deceased relatives, pets, or spiritual figures. The tunnel or corridor that many see is a passageway to a different realm or dimension.

In many cases they remember going through a review of their lives which gives them some understanding. Some say they meet a barrier which they see as the point of no return, and many are aware of a decision being taken to return to earth. Some see beings as soon as they come out of the body. In a significant number of cases the experience is an unpleasant one, even hellish.

These experiences are common throughout different cultures in the world, although there are differences in the details.

Most of the experiences are geared toward the individual, to what they understand of spirituality, and their life experience. But overall it is not a learnt cultural experience in itself.

Additionally, there are many cases of friends or relatives sensing the presence of a person who had just died as though they were trying to contact them.

It's common for people to have difficulty explaining their experience to others and a high proportion return from the experience with a belief in reincarnation or supernatural beings. Those who have had hellish NDEs almost always return with a sense of urgency about using their lives wisely and wanting to be close to divinity, even if they were atheists before it happened.

OBEs AS A WAY TO LEARN ABOUT NDEs

The study of near-death experiences from the three-dimensional world can bring some understanding of what they are and why they happen, but further exploration of this subject can be done by having clear and objective out-of-body experiences. If you do this, you can see people who have died and even watch as they go through the process of death out of the body. It's really quite difficult though to be able to travel not only out of the body, but also to explore death and other regions that exist there, and these kinds of experiences are usually given by spiritual beings to assist a person in their understanding of something that is important to them.

By having out-of-body experiences, it's possible to see things about death you had no prior knowledge of. You may even be able to read about them later not only in NDE research, but even in religious writings that are thousands of years old.

It's possible to see "ghosts" while you're in the astral plane, as over there you see ghosts as they are. In the physical world you may just feel or see some of their materializations, such as fleeting shadows, eerie feelings and the like—but there you can see what's causing these kinds of phenomena. I'd heard that an old school friend of mine had died in a motorbike accident; he had been dead for three days and that night I saw him while out of my body. Now without going into too much detail, ghosts are discarded mental forms, personalities that are unable to comprehend anything new—they are trapped in the past. When I saw my old friend I went closer to him but stopped. I was surprised to see that around him was an atmosphere of violence—you can feel these kinds of energies as a substance over there—it irradiated from him and became the element in which he existed. He turned toward me and I could see the violence in him, so I left his "ghost" to his world.

When back in the body I wondered about that emotion as I had not thought of him as a violent person, but looking back I began to see it. Then thinking about how he became a biker after leaving school, I realized that he lived with strong violent emotions, and this was his overriding psychological trait, which is why his ghost lived in that element after his death. I could have found out more about his character if I had observed his ghost longer or asked it questions, but I felt in that case that I had seen enough.

I realize that an account like this doesn't prove the existence of life after death to anyone else. Most experiences out of the body don't. But it is typical of what someone may find when encountering the figure of a deceased person, although the experience would of course vary according to the deceased, their personality, and their situation. It's more difficult to see the consciousness of the person who has died, especially when they have passed into a higher, more spiritual dimension: the sixth. It's more common to see their personality in the fifth.

CONSCIOUSNESS AS INDEPENDENT OF BRAIN ACTIVITY

Most scientists today would not take personal experience seriously, and yet are unable to explain nor offer a viable alternative to credible accounts that come from personal experiences and do offer convincing anecdotal evidence of life continuing after death. The majority of them believe that consciousness is entirely dependent on brain activity; however, they cannot explain how it exists in the absence of brain activity (as considerable anecdotal evidence shows that it does). Therefore the explanations lack credibility and what I said about scientific proof for out-of-body experiences applies here as well.

The fact that people can acquire information when their brain is dead and they're out of their body shows that consciousness is separate from the brain. Near-death experiences provide compelling anecdotal evidence of consciousness existing outside the brain, as they occur when the brain is not functioning—that's when actually dead rather than in pre-death shutdown or revival. Under these circumstances, there is simply no way that an OBE can be caused by any bodily function. Scientists cannot convincingly explain the case (just to take one example of many) of a woman who, after being brain and bodily dead and then revived by medical staff on an operating table, said after revival that she had been out of her body, went to the roof of the hospital, and saw a specific kind of shoe on the roof of the hospital. Medical staff then went to the roof and recovered the shoe, which was not visible from the ground, only from the air.

Some scientists accept that due to compelling accounts it is likely that near-death experiences show that consciousness exists outside the body, but say that ordinary out-of-body experiences are only subjective experiences in which the brain creates its own model of reality. This begs the question: at what point exactly does an NDE become an OBE? Logically, if you accept NDEs as showing the existence of consciousness beyond the body, then clearly OBEs could logically show the same thing. However, there seems to be a resistance in the scientific community to even speculate that this could be the case. I wonder if it's because if OBEs are found by academics to be objective experiences as most NDEs are, then OBEs become a valid way of getting more information about NDEs in ways that conventional science cannot replicate, use, or understand, and this would require too big a step beyond current scientific methodology to accept. Although the repercussions of accepting consciousness existing outside the body would be very challenging to science, it would probably rock the boat too much to even consider thinking outside the box. Unsurprisingly, there has been and continues to be very little research done into OBEs.

I was interviewed on BBC radio with a leading researcher into NDEs who is also a senior lecturer in psychiatry at a prominent London college and we disagreed about the objectivity of OBEs. Present in the interview was a lady who had been unconscious with an illness in hospital and while in that state she saw a doctor in a red turban (in the example I gave earlier in the book in the section on scientific proof for out-of body experiences). Although we both agreed that she technically had an OBE and not an NDE, I was dismayed at the professor's suggestion that it would be appropriate having had such an experience to seek psychiatric care. Science knows as little about consciousness as it does about OBEs, which is virtually nothing. It seems that for most part all science has to offer a person who wants to understand their NDE is another person with little or no OBE experience who will listen to them and who may prescribe them a pill.

Yet the same professor speaking at the International Association for Near-Death Studies (IANDS) annual conference stated, "Neuroscience has come up against a block. The problem is that neuroscientists do not know what consciousness is and have no theories to explain its nature. That is because our science is the science of the external world, a hangover from the time of the Renaissance, and it does not deal with subjective experience, or with consciousness. This is the main problem facing neuroscience at the moment, and it may well be that NDE research will be one way of filling the 'consciousness gap' in neuroscience."

I wouldn't hold your breath. Science generally is too rigid in its ways of thinking in this area and is highly unlikely to change its course anytime soon. It's another mistake too, to equate personal experience with subjective experience, since personal experience can be objective as well as subjective, but I wouldn't expect to see a rush of academics trying to work around it.

LEARNING ABOUT DEATH WITH ASTRAL PROJECTION

It's very enlightening to watch or read about people's own accounts of their near-death experiences; they show so much about the process that happens after death. It's a wonder more people don't look at them, since life is so temporary. But we can learn about the process of death through astral projection.

That's not to say we can expect to have an OBE and be given a guided tour of the process of death. We are often given the learning we need, not necessarily what we want to see. It's more likely that over time, through a series of OBEs, you'll have experiences here and there from which you'll be able to piece together parts of or much of the picture of death. This has been my experience, but then again you never know, you may be taught significantly in a single OBE.

You would have to be prepared too to learn some uncomfortable things. Those who have spiritual, loving NDEs seldom if ever get to experience the horrors of the Abyss, as they are in the process of learning from light and not darkness. But if you have an OBE, you will probably begin in what some in NDEs have described as the "copy world," which is the astral plane. But it can be unsettling to go from there into the hall of hell, which is purgatory, or into the Abyss itself, so if you were able to do that, you would have to be prepared for it.

Through many OBEs you'll probably get a sense of how life is a school, how it's a preparation for eternity, and how there are many lives for most people and not just a single one. Life is not an arbitrary material experience, nor is it a matter of just being in the here and now and experiencing what comes, believing everything will be fine.

It makes sense to use the time on earth wisely now, now that you're alive and have the opportunity, rather than putting your faith in others to tell you how to live. Find out for yourself what's going on—it will be too late when it's over. Scientists and the majority of people don't know the answers, they won't help you when your time has run out, and you alone will face the consequences of how you lived your life. And don't do or think in a certain way just because the majority of people do—the herd mentality won't help you. Anyway, it's futile to try to get widespread scientific acceptance for out-of-body experiences, no matter how compelling the account of the experience of the traveler. It remains for the individual to prove it for themselves.

It's clear that waiting for science to give all the answers in relation to out-of-body experiences is a waste of time. At the end of a lifetime's wait, very little if any progress will have been made, and if someone wishes to explore this subject, the only way is to listen to what others who have had them have to say, and personally have out-of-body experiences yourself and explore from there. It's up to you to decide to act or not. Ultimately, each of us stands alone upon the consequences of our own actions.

CHAPTER FOURTEEN

BRINGING THE MYSTERIES OF DREAMS AND OBEs INTO DAILY LIVING

IF YOU COMBINE ASTRAL TRAVEL with other spiritual exercises and live a spiritual life, you will find yourself in a magical world that is very different from an ordinary lifestyle.

It's worthwhile now and then taking some time to reflect upon your life and where it's going. Astral exercises fit right into a spiritual lifestyle and then daily life becomes an incredible adventure of learning and discovery.

If spirituality is not a priority, an effective astral program can still be created, but it's likely that spirituality would be discovered just through astral projection anyway. And spirituality has more to do with what is experienced than what is merely believed, so it's best to keep an open mind. Spirituality is a wide-ranging term that means different things to different people; I take it in a broad sense of the experience of a reality beyond the material.

A life lived without spiritual experience tends to be divorced from the astral world, which often becomes little more than a hobby.

Astral explorations are most effective when part of a spiritual way of living, and then they tend to have greater meaning and significance.

What is thought of and desired throughout the day directs both internal and external life. And, regardless of what a person believes themselves to be, what they really are is manifested in what they actually think, feel, and do.

In taking spirituality as a lifestyle, astral programs can be created with clear goals and they integrate into a lifestyle. It's then easier to think about doing astral exercises, to be more aware, to remember to practice throughout the day, and to direct daily activities toward spiritual development, which gives much greater ability to succeed with astral exercises.

For those whom spiritual development is a priority, I would advise making use of the events in life to learn about yourself and to awaken consciousness. In using each moment and living each day with the spiritual as the main center of focus, drive, and interest, your life will be transformed.

GETTING KNOWLEDGE THE WAY ANCIENT MYSTICS DID

Using lucid dreams and having out-of-body experiences with astral projection offers a way to explore what happens to us when we dream, have OBEs, and die, that is far more effective than conventional science can offer.

The combined scientific study in all fields including physics, medicine, psychology, neuroscience, psychiatry, and even parapsychology have failed to answer basic questions about what it is to be human, such as what consciousness is, what dreams and their functions are, and what out-of-body and near-death experiences are.

These are basic human questions, and they have not even remotely begun to be answered because they are nonphysical phenomena and science uses an ineffective criterion of purely physical verification that has to be experienced by all. This is why "officially" so little is known about what happens to us in the time we spend out of our bodies.

This is instead a return to ancient learning methods, in which you study yourself. Your own personal experience when dreaming, having emotions, out-of-body experiences, etc., is by its nature experienced personally, and can be most effectively studied at an individual basis through the application of the correct techniques of inner study.

As the human psyche is essentially similar between all individuals, by studying ourselves, we see how other people work psychologically too.

DREAMS AND OBEs FOR SELF-KNOWLEDGE

If you want to find out how a fruit tastes that you have never tried before, do you just read other people's accounts of what it tasted like to them, or study the biological responses to eating, or study people's behavior when eating the fruit? It's unlikely. Instead, you'll probably pick up the fruit (assuming you know it's safe) bite into it, and chew it.

In the same way, if you want to know something about yourself such as how anger works, you can look inside to see it within yourself when you get angry. You can see how it actually feels, what it makes you do, what triggers it off, how it appears in your dreams, and so on.

In this way you'll learn about how anger functions for you and will get knowledge about it; this kind of knowledge is often referred to as "self-knowledge." With this knowledge you can even understand and reduce the undesirable psychological states within yourself such as fear, anxiety, misery, etc., and get to better states such as peace. In so doing, you'll also reduce those undesirable states in your dreams as they are directly related to how a person feels in the day. The nature of dreams therefore changes and they become more pleasant.

Sleep is an extremely valuable spiritual asset that you can use to your advantage if you want to and know how to. If you study your dreams you can find information about yourself, and when combined with lucid dreaming and out-of-body experiences, you have excellent tools for self-discovery. If in your daily life you observe and study yourself, see how you act, feel, think, etc., you can also learn about those same things in your dreams. As you change in daily life, then so do dreams change, and self-study in daily life, dream recall, and OBEs become mutually sustaining ways to real and lasting change.

SPIRITUAL DEVELOPMENT AND OBEs

The kinds of out-of-body experiences we have is important; it's one thing to just get into the astral plane, but it's another to be developing spiritually. Anyone can fly around and explore the astral world, but few actually penetrate its deeper secrets. To do that requires a level of spiritual preparedness.

Many people like to dabble and experiment here and there, and will move on from astral projection to other exercises and spiritual practices, while others will be happy to read a little then go on to reading something else, watching videos, while adding to their intellectual knowledge, but missing out on any consistent personal experience of higher worlds. Some however, will want to explore deeper into the nature of themselves and life and walk the spiritual path.

PAINTING IN CHANGCHUN TEMPLE, WUHAN

There's so much more to learn than you can get from having simple astral experiences, and so much knowledge to discover. Being in the astral plane is a way to get a certain level of knowledge, but if you don't become an initiate of the spiritual path, you will never get advanced knowledge or wisdom. You will only get incipient, basic, and often inaccurate information, and will have to muddle your way through a complex web of experiences that you have little way of understanding.

CONCLUSION

Out-of-body experiences are the means to travel to other dimensions where there are different realms in which other forms of life exist.

These other dimensions are where we came from before we were born and where we return to after death. We also visit them every time we dream.

They are the source of the supernatural, and in them are found the origins of the religions and myths that have been passed down to us through the passage of time.

Beyond the dimensions is the source of our origin as consciousness and the destination of enlightenment.

By traveling out of the body we can know of the purpose to life, and how to use it wisely. We can follow the steps to enlightenment, gain immense knowledge and spiritual experience, and can contact other beings.

If you do acquire some of this knowledge, help yourself in your personal spiritual awakening, but use it to help others, and contribute to the good of individuals, society, and humanity; nothing exists in isolation and we are all part of the same source.

MysticalLifePublications.org

For more works by Belsebuub,
visit his official website

BELSEBUUB.COM

.

CPSIA information can be obtained
at www.ICGtesting.com
Printed in the USA
BVHW01s0738011217
501667BV00003B/314/P